# *Gardening Indoors with HID Lights*

by George F. Van Patten

Alyssa F. Bust

Published by Van Patten Publishing
Cover Design: Tin Man Design
Artwork: Hart James
Book Design: G. F. Van Patten
Cover Photo: Courtesy of Jane Flanders, Paul Cronk, Hygrotech and Don Masey Orchids.- The Patented Adjust-A-Shade reflector in the cover photo was developed by Paul Cronk, Australia. In Australia, the reflector is known as Adjust-A-Shade. In North America and Europe it is called Adjust-A-Wing.

Back Cover Photos are compiled from various sources.
Copyright 1997, George F. Van Patten
ISBN 1-878823-20-5
First Printing
9 8 7 6 5 4 3 2 1

This book is written for the purpose of supplying gardening informa-tion to the public. It is sold with the agreement that it does not offer any guarantee of plant growth or well-being. Readers of this book are responsible for all plants cultivated. You are encouraged to read any and all information available about indoor gardening and gardening in general to develop a complete background on these subjects so you can tailor this information to your individual needs. This book should be used as a general guide to gardening indoors, as not the ultimate source.

The authors and Van Patten Publishing have tried to the best of their abilities to describe all of the most current methods used to garden successfully indoors. However, there may be some mistakes in the text that the authors and publisher were unable to detect. This book contains current information up to the date of this publication.

Neither the publisher nor the authors endorse any products or brand names that are mentioned or pictured in the text. These products are pictured or mentioned for illustration only.

**To the Editors:**
We want to thank each one of you. With your help, knowledge and perserverence, this book is possible.

AUSTRALIA - Grant Creevy, Paul Cronk, Robin Moseby, Vivian Ireland, South Pacific, Gramme Plummer, Mariee

CANADA - Guy Dionne, Solar Greenhouse Burnaby, BC, AJ Hamilton's buddy, Frank Pastor, Don Stewart, Tim Walker, William Sutherland, Francois Wolf, Jr., Kelly Zastownie,

UNITED KINGDOM - Giles Gunstone,

USA - Carl Anderson, Tom Alexander, Russ Antkowiak, Joen Belanger, Larry Brooke, Michael Christain, Harmon Davidson, Tom Duncan, Ed German, Jeff Gibson, Kim Hanna, Richard Holland, Tim Hydrofarm, David Ittel, Steve Lees, Dan Lubkeman, Rick Martin, Carl McLaughlin, Richard Middlebrook, Rajem Purcifel, Mark Rambod, Bill ross, Craig Ryan, Judy Ryan, Roger Thayer, Tom Shelsky, Jeanie Shelsky, Steve Smith, Steve Stragnola, David Strong, Jerry Vandenberg, Patrick Vivian, Brent Walker, Peter Wardenberg,,


**Special thanks** to: Dan Lubkeman, Giles Gunstone, Peter Wardenberg, Paul Cronk

This book is dedicated to the Plant a Row for the Hungry Program. This wonderful program has been growing rapidly across America and we would like to see it grow worldwide. The premise is simple, plant one extra row or bed in your garden and give it to hungry people.

Your local telephone book has the names of several agencies, such as Second Harvest, that will help you distribute your bounty.

**Plant a Row for the Hungry!**

# Table of Contents

# Introduction

Light is one of many environmental factors that determines plant growth. When gardening indoors, hobbyists and professionals alike assume the responsibilities of Mother Nature. Indoor gardeners must regulate water, fertilizer, humidity, nutrients, carbon dioxide, heat and light in order to promote optimum growth. Until recently, gardeners knew how to best regulate all of these factors except one: light. Accepting that they could not control the sun's cycles, gardeners resigned themselves to losses during winter months. Through research and experimentation, however, artificial lights have made it possible for gardeners to control lighting. In fact, gardeners can so accurately control all the factors which contribute to plant life that an indoor garden can flourish even in an isolated, windowless basement.

The development of artificial light technology has had clear benefits for production growers. Production growers have been able to improve the quality of their vegetables and flower crops, better utiling outdoor field and greenhouse space, extend plant longevity and synchronize plant maturity with market demand. Artificial lights allow gardeners to force flowering according to seasonal demand. A blooming poinsettia or Christmas cactus, for instance, islikely to sell better in December than in July.

The benefits of artificial lighting are not exclusive to the professional gardener. Home hobbyists also reap the benefits of flexibility, control and increased plant health. An otherwise unusable dark basement corner can be converted into a garden room with a small investment. In fact, you can set up an indoor garden area anywhere in your home provided that the air temperature remains between 65 and 75 degrees (18-24 degrees C). Artificial lights can be used to highlight an already flourishing plant collection, or to promote growth in a new or struggling species. Lights can be installed in a garden area (be it a single bank of fluorescents in the corner of a kitchen, or an entire room in a basement or heated garage), or throughout your living space to help nourish individual plants.

This book is about artificial light. In the first chapter, you will find general information about light and its relationship to plant health. In the second chapter, we discuss various sources of light, including sunlight and artificial light. The third chapter provides information on incandescent, tungsten halogen and fluorescent bulbs. The forth chapter focuses on high intensity discharge (HID) lights and their horticultural applications. Because there are many kinds of artificial lights from which to choose, we provide easy to use reference charts which highlight the advantages and detriments of different lamps and reflective hoods. The last two chapters provide you with the electrical and technical details that will allow you to safely install and maintain a lighting system. At the end of the book, you will find several appendices that cover more details on lamps and plant lighting. In short, our goal is to serve as a resource to help you get the most out of your garden. This book will help you make wise light-investment choices because each penny you invest in lighting can provide you with great results in plant growth.

Note: We make many recommendations in this book some recommendations are based upon experience or empirical observation and others based upon manufacturers specifications.

# Chapter One: Light and Its Relationship to Plants

## Light Basics

Understanding light, what it is, and how it works, is essential to gardeners because light provides the energy which stimulates plant growth. Although we tend to take it for granted, light is a building block of life on Earth. Plants rely on light to produce food and maintain healthy growth and flowering. From a gardener's perspective, light is one of many environmental factors that determine plant health. From a technical or scientific stand-point, light is just one form of radiant energy (See Appendix A). It is important for gardeners to have a general understanding of the scientific considerations of light so that they can use it efficiently in their gardens. Having developed an understanding of the basic characteristics of light, it is then possible to apply that knowledge to horticulture. In this chapter, you will find a discussion of how light affects plant health and how you can best utilize it to regulate photosynthesis, phototropism and photoperiodism. In order to use light effectively, you need to know how to measure it and how and when to employ the use of artificial light. This chapter will help you develop the knowledge you need to begin successfully using light effectively in your garden.

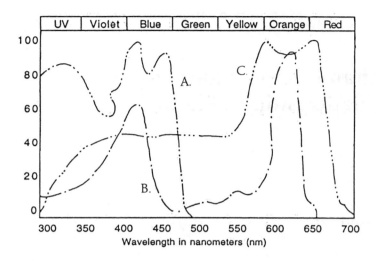

*This Photosynthetic Response Chart shows the levels of sunlight that are needed for specific plant processes. A is the phototropic response, B: chlorophyll synthsis, C: photosynthetic response*

Light quality and quantity are the dominant factors affecting several important plant processes including photosynthesis, phototropism and photoperiodism. Of these, photosynthesis is the most important as it is the basis of plant and ultimately human life. Plants use light to produce food and support growth. Although plants are the only organism that can convert light into food, all living species depend on light for life. Plants depend on it directly, animals and humans indirectly. When you consume plants or animals (who have consumed plants) you are also consuming the light energy used by the plants to produce food. When gardening indoors under artificial lights, it is important to maximize the benefits of the light you provide to your garden. You can do this by understanding how and when plants use specific areas of the light spectrum.

## Light and Plant Processes:

What humans see as colors*, plants see as stimulants to food production, flowering, dormancy, seed germination, chlorophyll manufacturing, branching and leaf thickening. In addition, plants also respond to a wider spectrum of light than do humans. Plants utilize radiant energy from 280-800 nanometers,** while humans can detect only from 380-760nm (See Appendix A). Although plants utilize a wider spectrum, they do so selectively. (See chart on Photosynthetic Response).

Although light is a crucial element in many plant processes, not all frequencies of light affect plants equally. For instance, photosynthesis is stimulated by both red and blue light, while photoperiodism is governed only by red and far-red wavelengths. The blue and blue-green range of the spectrum stimulates the greatest phototropic response. Red light, on the other hand, does not initiate any phototropic response. Each plant variety may respond a little diffrently to each color of the light spectrum. Photochromes (growth-promoting chemicals found in plants) utilize either red or far red light. For this reason, you must experiment with specific varieties of plants to find which grow the best under a specific light. (see also Appendix B: Light Requirements of Plants). The relationship between the blue and red light Phytochromes (growth promoting chemicals found in plants) utilize either red or far-red light. Red energy also stimulates seed germination, seedling and vegetative growth, cell and organ elongation and flowering. Blue light,

*Plants and humans use different parts of light. Plants use photons which carry energy, while humans use waves to see their environment in color. People use photons directly also. Light photons striking our skin (sunlight and tanning lights) produce vitamin A, D & E, vital to our health.
**One nanometer (nm) = one billionth of a meter)

on the other hand, inhibits cell and organ elongation. Understanding that different color lights stimulate different plant responses allows gardeners to accurately control plant growth. Some gardeners, strive to achieve a mix of blue and red light while others alternate between the two or use one exclusively.

## Photosynthesis

Light is a crucial ingredient in a plant's recipe for food. In fact, the word photosynthesis comes from the Greek word for light, photos. Plants are able to use light largely because of activity that happens in their leaves. Leaves are the work horses of plants; they absorb light and convert it into usable food. Pigments and chloroplasts in leaf cells collect light energy. Chlorophyll, the substance which makes leaves green, is a pigment. Leaves look green because they reflect light energy which is that frequency or color. While rejecting green light, chlorophyll absorbs red and blue light. Only after the chlorophyll has absorbed the light can the energy from the photons be utilized. Once in the leaf cells, this light energy fuels many plant processes, the most important of which is photosynthesis. During photosynthesis, plants convert radiant energy (light) into chemical energy (food). They knit together carbon dioxide from the air and water and inorganic material from the soil to produce carbohydrates and sugars. In essence, light energy is transferred into energy-rich molecules, including ATP (adenosine-derived nucleotide) and sugar and then these molecules are transported to all parts of the plant, including its roots, stems, flowers and growing areas. The energy is used and stored in the form of starches, fats and sugars. The sugars serve as the basis of growth because they are made into building materials (cellulose and others). Oxygen is released as a by-product. At night, photosynthesis stops and plants absorb oxygen and emit carbon dioxide in a process known as respiration. During respiration, plants produce proteins and other complex products that can not be produced during photosynthesis. (See chart on Photosynthetic Response).

## Photoperiodism

Light also affects plant growth through a process known as photoperiodism. The length of daylight, known as the photoperiod, determines flowering, seed formation, stem lengthening, leaf growth and color and bulb and tuber formation. It is actually the absence of light that determines these plant growth factors. Contrary to previous belief, scientists have now proven that the duration of darkness, not light, stimulates plant functions. Plants possess a flowering hormone known as florigen that can be destroyed if it is exposed to excessive light. Plants require a critical amount of florigen in order to flower. Too little florigen will not induce flowering while too much prevents blooming.

Historically plants have been classified according to the amount of daylight they require. Long-day plants such as grasses, grains, most vegetables and most annuals, require 14-18 hours of light to accumulate optimum amounts of florigen. Short-day plants such as Napa cabbages, poinsettias, chrysanthemum and gardenias rely on 10-13 hours of light to produce florigen. Long-day/short-day plants such as China astors (*Callistephus Sinensis*), require a specific light cycle of long days followed by short days to bloom. Day-neutral plants are theoretically not effected by the duration of light. However, day-neutral plants may flower more with more light because of increases in photosynthesis. In addition, day-neutral plants are sensitive to day and night tem-

perature variations. This is called thermo-periodism.
Turning off lamps at night decreases the air temperature
which triggers flowering.

Although many gardeners still classify their plants
according to daylight requirements, it is more accurate to
classify them according to darkness requirements. Short-day
plants are actually long-night plants and long-day plants are
actually short-night plants. If even a minimal amount of
light interrupts the dark period of long-night plants, their
flowering can be stunted. Many gardeners use short bursts
of light to interrupt darkness delay flowering and control
growth. When possible, it is best to group plants together
according to their daylight requirements.

Plant varieties also vary as to their exact response to
photoperiod length. Scientific data is limited on the *exact*
response of many plants to these factors.


## Phototropism

Phototropism is also determined by light.
Phototropism is the term that describes a plant's reaction to
light when it is not equally distributed or received on all
sides of a plant. Plants respond to light by moving towards
or away from it. Positive tropism is when a plant or a part of
a plant bends towards the light. Negative tropism indicates
that the plant is growing away from the light. Sunflowers got
their name because they follow the course of the sun
throughout the day. In the morning, their heads turn
towards the east and in the evening they turn to the west.
For optimum growth, provide evenly distributed light to your
garden. In Chapter Four you will find a discussion of how to
employ light movers and reflective light to help ensure even
light distribution.

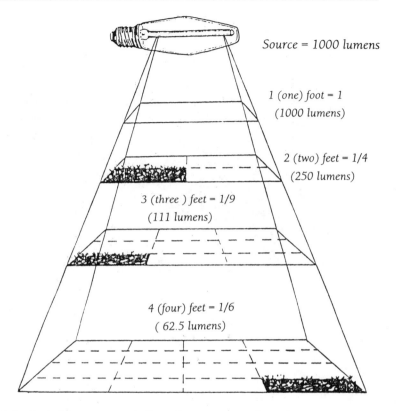

*Light diminishes exponentially as it moves away from the source.*

## Light Intensity

Plants discriminate not only by light color, but also by light intensity. Intensity measures quantity of light energy per unit of time. Light intensity requirements vary with plant species. Outdoors, plants grow under a wide range of light intensities, from 10 to 10,000 foot-candles. Plants that prefer low light intensities naturally grow in the shade while those that require high intensities grow in full sun. You have probably considered light intensity in your own gardening, both indoors and outdoors. Certain houseplants grow better on a sunny windowsill while others thrive in a dark corner.

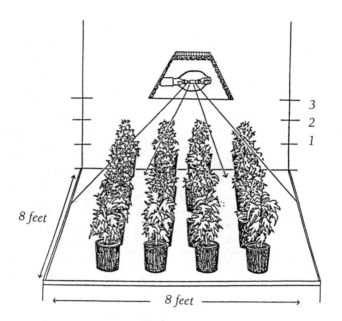

*Intense light penetrates plants heavy foliage so all leaves are active..*

 **Rule of Thumb:** Light intensity diminishes *very* quickly! The closr a lamp is to plants the more light plants receive.

With an understanding of light intensity, it is possible to employ artificial lights successfully. In fact, you can control light so successfully that it is possible to grow robust plants in the complete absence of sunlight.

The first and foremost quality of artificial light is that it fades fast. *Artificial light fades very fast.* To overcome fast fading light you can:

1. Choose a bright light
2. Choose an efficient reflective hood
3. Choose a reflective hood with even light distribution
4. Choose a reflective hood that can be placed as close

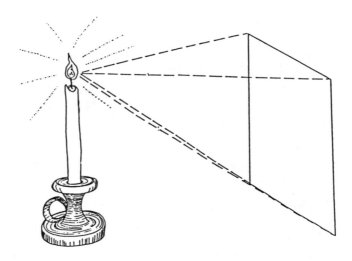

*One foot-candle is the amount of radiant light from a standard candle that falls on one square foot of surface area at a distance of one foot.*

as possible to the garden without burning plants.
5. Maintain short plants (2-3 feet) so the light penetrates the foliage.

## Measuring Light

When choosing a lighting system for your indoor garden, pay attention to how much light is emitted by the lighting system and how much light is *received* by the plants. We have learned that light intensity decreases *very* rapidly as you move away from the source. Plants grown on the outside of a lighted area receive less intense light than those grown directly below the source.

To determine the light intensity in different areas, you will need to measure the light received at plant level (See Appendix A). Most common light measurement devices read

## How to Use a Light Meter

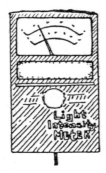 

*This light meter is the most important indoor garden tool. High-light plants require 50,000 (4,650 fc) to 80,000 lux (7,500 fc). Mid day sun at the equator is 100,000 lux. Do not garden without one!*

Using a light meter is simple and the information you gather with it will keep your light shinning as bright as possible. We prefer hand-held light metersthat you use to take simple readings at different places under the bulb. Our favorite way to use a light meter is to cut a piece of string 3 feet long. Attach this string to one of the corners of the light hood with a piece of tape. Extend the piece of string to three feet directly below the hood and take a measurement. This is not the distance from the bulb, but will serve as a good reminder and starting point to make measurements. You can also take measurements at different angles under the reflective hood. We suggest that you take measurements under the hood monthly. You will find that your bulb diminishes in intensity each month. When it falls to a point of supplying less light than your garden needs, move the lamp closer or change bulbs.

*This gardener uses a 3-foot string to measure the amount of light plants receive at 3 feet. He holds the string straight and puts the light meter at the end of the string.*

in either foot-candles or lux. (one lux = 10.76 footcandles). Our explanations and examples will use footcandles and convert to lux.

The foot-candle is an easy-to-understand unit of measurement with which most people are familiar. We can use foot-candles to determine how much light is received by plants. (see also Appendix A, Measuring Light)

You can use a photographic light meter on a camera to measure light intensities for low-light plants and then convert the reading into foot-candles. Set the film speed (ASA) to 200 and the shutter speed to 1/125 second. Place a piece of white paper in the garden area you are measuring. Stand close enough to the paper so that it is all you can see through the lens. Adjust the camera lens aperture (f stop) until the light meter reads a correct exposure. Calculate foot-candles using the following chart.

**Lens aperture = foot-candles**

| | | | |
|---|---|---|---|
| f4 | = | 64 f.c. | = 688 lux |
| f5.6 | = | 125 f.c | = 1345 lux |
| f8 | = | 250 f.c. 2 | = 690 lux |
| f11 | = | 500 f.c. 5 | = 380 lux |
| f16 | = | 1000 f.c. | = 10760 lux |
| f22 | = | 2000 f.c | = 21520 lux |

**Rule of Thumb:** Multiply foot-candles by 10.76 = luc

1000 foot-candles x 10.76 = 10760

Pocket-size light meters which read directly in foot-candles are available at garden supply and hardware stores. Many of these instruments have a range of 0 to more than 1000 foot-candles. As a general rule, the more expensive the light meter, the more accurate and the greater the range it will measure.

**Rule of Thumb:** Buy a light meter and measure your light output at least once a month.

One way to measure light intensity, or quantity, is in watts-per-square foot. All bulbs are rated according to the watts. For comparing lamps and their energy distribution, measuring watts-per-square-meter provides a good place to start. (To convert watts-per-square-meter to watts-per-square-foot replace 1 meter with 3.28 feet) Watts-per-square-meter does not address the lumens-per-watt generated by bulbs, nor does it measure the amount of light a horizontal compared to a vertical bulb/reflector generates. Watts-per-square-meter measurements do not account for the height of the lamp above plants either. But watts-per-square-meter measurements do make it easy to calculate your lighting costs per square meter.

To determine watts-per-square-meter, first determine how many square meters your garden occupies. To do this, multiply length by width. If your growing area is two meters by two meters, it is 4 square meters. Now divide the total wattage of your light fixture by the square meters of your growing area. If you are using a 1,000 watt lamp, divide 1,000 watts by 4 square meters. 1,000/ 4 = 250 watts-per-square-meter.

**Total watts of light**

---

**Square meters in garden area (length X width)**

**= watts-per-square-meter**

To convert the above example into watts-per-square foot, replace 1 meter with 3.28 feet. For example: 2 meters = 6.56 feet. 6.56 feet x 6.56 feet = 40.03 square feet. 1000 watts divided by 40.03 square feet = 24.98 watts-per-square foot. Cross reference this information with the information in Appendix B: Light Requirements of Plants.

Provided that your lamp is a prescribed distance from the plant tops, your garden area will receive 250 watts of light for every square meter (24.98 watts-per-square foot). Most gardeners hang a 400 watt lamp about one foot above plant tips. To increase the intensity, you can use higher wattage lamps, or you can lower the lamps so that there is less room between the lamp and the plant tips. To avoid burning plant tips, do not position high intensity discharge lamps (HID) too close to your plants. Always watch for signs of burning: darkened leaves that are closest to the bulb. Fluorescent lamps, because they do not get as hot as their HID counterparts, are hardly a threat.

To decrease light intensity, move the lamp farther away from the plants. A lamp hung twenty-four inches from the plants will provide approximately one quarter the light intensity compared with one hung at twelve inches. When

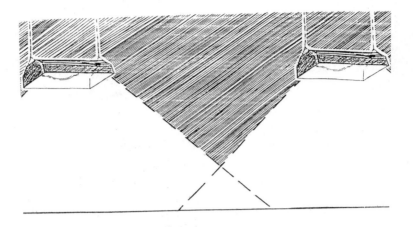

*Two lights with overlapping lumens. The sum of the lumens in the overlapping areas equals total lumens.*

more than one fixture is used, light intensity diminishes less rapidly with distance due to the added fixtures.

To measure light intensity without a light meter, you can use characteristics of the plant to make an educated guess. Elongated stems, pale green or colorless leaves and leaves which will not expand properly indicate a lack of sufficiently balanced light. Pale yellow or green leaves, stems which do not elongate, red leaves that do not expand properly and leaves that burn or get crispy can be characteristics of exposure to excess light.

Plants all have a minimum light requirement (see Appendix B: Light Requirements of Plants). Remember, light is ultimately a source of plant food. You can think of light in terms of calories. Calories measure the energy content in human food. Individual calorie needs vary depending on size, metabolism and activity rate. Similarly each plant type has its own minimum light requirement. Remember, if your

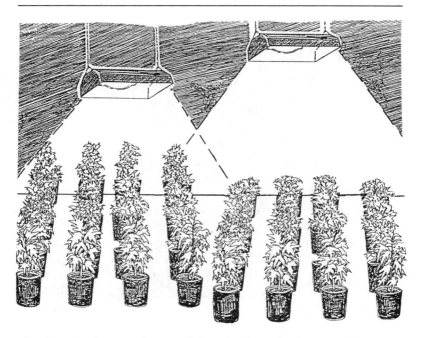

*One lamp is closer to plants and the other lamp farther away demonstrates how much more intense light plants receive when the lamp is closer.*

plants are too crowded, they will shade one another. Shaded plants receive less light than others. If you rely on natural light to meet your compensation point, remember that light intensity varies for different climate conditions and seasons. Cloudy days provide low light intensities. In the winter, light intensity may drop to as low as 22 percent of its June high. This change of intensity is due to the earth's tilt. In the summer, light is going through only one or two thicknesses of atmosphere. In the winter, when the sun is low on the horizon, the light has to travel through four or five thicknesses of atmosphere at noon. While the reverse is true in Australia and the Southern Hemisphere, this seasonal difference in light intensity is negligible near the equator. A study conducted in Pennsylvania revealed that light intensity is less

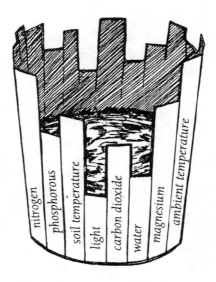

*Plants will grow as fast as the limiting factor allows.*

than its summer high for a significant portion of the year. If you base the June light intensity at 100, it is 50 in October, 28 in November, 22 in December, 25 in January, 37 in February and 54 in March. If you garden indoors, you must compensate for low light intensities using artificial lights.

To get the most from your lighting dollars, you must know when to apply different light intensities. For germinating seeds and rooting cuttings, use 10 lamp watts-per-square foot of garden area. For example, a Gro-Lux lamp should be 1-6 inches above plants. For low-light plants, including many houseplants, provide 100-300 foot-candles. Secure a light source such as a 400 watt horizontal super metal halide 3-5 feet above the plants. Medium light plants should receive 300-500 For high-light plants, use a light level of at least 500 foot-candles. Hang a 1000 watt horizontal HID 2 feet above or a 400 watt horizontal HID 1 foot above plant tips. Roses, carnations, chrysanthemums, tomatoes, beans and many vegetables are high-light plants. (see Appendix B for specific recommendations on plants).

Another way to look at this concept with daylight neutral plants such as lettuce is to understand foot-candle hours, the amount of total foot-candles in relation to the hours one foot-candle shines on a garden. For example, a garden that receives 1000 foot-candles for one hour receives 1000 foot-candle hours - 1000 foot-candles for two hours receives 2000 foot-candle hours - 1000 foot-candles for three hours receives 3000 foot-candle hours. A salad garden that gets less light in an artificial light garden than it would if it received sunlight can still grow excellent salad. If this garden receives 5000 foot-candles per hour for 8 hours outdoors (total 40,000 fc hours) it would receive almost the same amount of light from 2000 fc for 18 hours (total = 36000 fc hours). Remember, this example is only good for day neutral plants.

# Chapter Two:
# Sunlight and
# Artificial Light

Having established the importance of light and its relationship to plants, you must now consider what kind of light you want to employ in your garden area. In this chapter we will explore the difference between sunlight and artificial light. When you choose to use artificial light, you want to ensure that you get the highest return on your investment. This chapter focuses on several techniques you can employ to increase the benefits you receive from your lights. Understanding the benefits and disadvantages of both natural and artificial light will help you determine when and how to use them, individually and simultaneously.

## Sunlight

Utilizing sunlight for your indoor garden also has several benefits. For a gardener on a budget, the sun's greatest asset is that it is free. The sun emits radiant energy covering the entire range of the visible spectrum. Although the sun's light appears white, it is actually a blend of all colors. Because plants employ energy primarily in the red and blue ranges, most artificial lights concentrate on one of these two colors. None provide an ideal balance, but metal halides come very close. Gardeners are therefore often forced to use different lamps for different stages of plant growth to achieve optimum lighting. Although the sun provides much wasted light in the orange, yellow and green ranges, it is at least wasted light for which you do not have to pay.

Utilizing sunlight for indoor gardening has several disadvantages. Unlike artificial lights, it is difficult to control the sun's energy and its intensity. Sunlight varies drastically in intensity depending on time of year, cloud cover and air pollution. Relying on the sun as your energy source also means you need a convenient light-filled area in your home that can easily be converted into an indoor garden. For some, this is practical. If you are interested in creating a small garden area, or using a windowsill, you may be able to find a sunny spot in your home. Perhaps you are interested in lighting for a single plant in your living space. In this case, you may be able to position the plant in sufficient sunlight. However, many hobbyists want more room for their gardens than their living space allow. Heated garages and basements are therefore popular gardening locations. These locations allow you to expand your hobby as desired. In addition, many gardeners prefer to keep the soil, water, fertilizers and perhaps even carbon dioxide generators or emitters that go along with indoor gardening out of their living areas. The drawback of utilizing basements and garages for gardening is, of course, the lack of sunlight in these areas. So for many, employing sunlight as a primary source of light is neither practical nor sufficient.

It is, however, wise for all gardeners to make use of this free source of energy whenever possible. Take a reading of the sunlight in your garden area. Perhaps you will find that it is sufficient for some purposes. If you grow low-light plants, perhaps you receive enough sunlight to avoid artificial lights. Or perhaps you can rely on the sun as your primary light source for seedlings and cuttings. For the most part, however, even if you can utilize the sun for some lighting purposes, it probably will not meet all of your gardening needs. After all, even short-day plants require 10-13 hours of light per day. Unless you live in a climate where the sun always shines, it is unlikely that you will be able to consistently fulfill this need when relying solely on the sun.

## Artificial Light

Until relatively recently, gardeners suffered losses during the winter due to the predicament discussed above. During the winter not only are days shorter, but the sun's light is also less intense because the sun sits lower in the sky and is more likely to be covered by clouds. This combination made it impossible to maintain healthy crops during the winter. In fact, for 4-6 months a year, sunlight shortage and fowl weather restrict plant growth. Now, with increased ease and accessibility, hobby gardeners can maintain gardens regardless of the season by using artificial lights.

Many gardeners misunderstand the purpose of artificial lights. Artificial lights are not intended to duplicate sunlight. This would be impractical considering that the sun emits a large amount of wasted energy. Instead, artificial lamps attempt to produce the energy which is most used by plants in the blue and red ranges. For gardeners who can utilize sunlight, artificial lights supplement the sun's energy. Remember, the sun is free. If you can employ its energy, your budget will benefit. If you receive adequate sunlight, there is no need to supplement the sun's energy during daylight hours.

Another benefit of artificial light is the flexibility it provides. Using artificial light allows you to control growth and flowering. By interrupting dark periods with short bursts of light, you can prevent short-day plants from blooming and thereby maintain a schedule to your liking. Conversely, short-day plants such as poinsettias absolutely need 12 hours of darkness to force flowering at Christmas time. Even the slightest flicker of light can set flowering back a full day. It has been reported that fluorescent lights can give a brief flicker when they're off, enough to delay poinsettias. This flicker may be caused by police or aircraft radar, garage door openers or lightning in the vicinity. Although it would be convenient, the sun is not turned on by a timer or a switch and therefore does not provide you with this flexibility. The flexibility has been a huge boon for the professional horticulturists who can now match their plants' schedules with market needs. The benefits extend to hobby gardeners who can plan and control the schedules of their vegetable and flower gardens.

# Chapter Three:
# High Intensity Discharge Lamps

      Hobby gardeners have found that high intensity discharge lamps grow great gardens.  This chapter focuses on high intensity discharge (HID) lights including metal halide, high pressure (HP) sodium, retrofit conversion, mercury vapor and low pressure (LP) sodium bulbs.  We provide easy reference charts which compare the bulbs on the basis of their lumen-per-watt conversion, lumen maintenance, mortality hours, Kelvin temperature and cost per watt.

      To propagate and grow short low light plants, fluorescents are a good choice, but HIDs out-perform fluorescents with lumen-per-watt efficiency, spectral balance and brilliance.  If you want to grow any large or high-light plants, you need the brightness of HIDs.  Although HIDs are the preferred light of most indoor gardeners, they do have a few drawbacks.  HIDs often have a high initial cost.  Not only can the system itself be expensive, but you might also incur indirect costs.  HID systems produce heat and can require a fan or cooling system, especially if you garden in a small space.

      Several different bulbs comprise the high intensity discharge family.  In this chapter you will be introduced to the mercury vapor, metal halide, high pressure (HP) sodium, low pressure (LP) sodium and conversion bulbs, plus the experimental sulfur bulb.  We also briefly discuss other

bulbs including incandescents, tungsten halogens and fluorescents. Each has its own advantages and disadvantages
depending largely on your garden room needs. Some gardeners use different members of the HID family together to
produce more full light and to perform more diverse functions.

Although different HID bulbs perform different functions and emit light from different regions of the spectrum,
for the most part they create light in the same way. HIDs
work by passing electricity through vaporized gas under
high pressure. Low-pressure (LP) sodium lamps create light
by passing electricity through vaporized gas under *low* pressure. The gas is kept within a quartz glass or ceramic arc
tube and sealed under high pressure. Different colors are
produced by different bulbs depending on the materials
which are sealed in the arc tube. The arc tube is housed
within a larger outer bulb. A fair amount of UV is generated
by the inner bulb but filtered by the outer one.

CAUTION! If the outer shell (envelope) breaks on
HID bulbs, they may not go out. Turn off immediately and
DO NOT LOOK AT THE ARC TUBE WHEN LIT! Severe eye
damage can occur. Harmful ultraviolet (UV) light is being
emitted! Severe eye damage and skin burn can occur!

You can purchase an HID system at many specialty
garden supply stores or directly from a retailer. We advise to
buy your entire HID lighting system at the same time and
from the same supplier. A lighting system should include a
ballast, lamp, socket, bulb and reflector. Mismatched components are not efficient, usually will not work and are
potentially dangerous. When purchasing the system, make
sure it includes a written guarantee for at least a year.

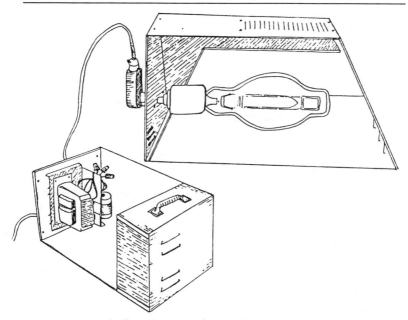

*A HID system - ballast, lamp, socket, bulb and reflector. The multi-tap transformer has four tabs, one for each voltage: 120, 208, 240 and 277*

**Rule of Thumb:** Buy the complete HID system from a reputable supplier.

All HID lamps require ballasts. Metal halide ballast boxes contain a capacitor and a transformer. HP sodium ballast boxes contain a capacitor, transformer and ignitor.

Note: The Iwasaki "Ignitron" HP sodium bulb contains the ignitor inside the bulb. If you use this bulb, the starter in the ballast must be disconnected.

Some smaller HIDs (below 100 watts) have electronic ballasts. Manufacturers are working ondeveloping electronic ballasts for larger watt HIDs, but have yet to do so. The advantages of electronic ballasts include heat, noise and electricity consumption reduction. Most 150, 175, 250 and some 400-watt systems contain their ballasts in one fixture with the reflective hood. For the most part, gardeners prefer

400, 600 and 1000 watt lamps that have remote ballasts. Metal halides are also available in 1500-watt bulbs. These bulbs are best suited for stadium lighting and produce too much heat to be practical for indoor gardening. Industrial high-bay ballasts that are attached to the reflector and socket and are not recommended for gardening purchases because they are heavy, difficult to mount properly and use extra ceiling (growing) height. The ballast is responsible for starting the lamps by providing a high, fast charge of electricity. After the bulb lights, the range of voltage and current are controlled by the transformer so the bulb functions efficiently.

Ballasts can be purchased either assembled or unassembled. If you are not a qualified electrician with formal training we recommend that you purchase an assembled unit. Ballasts are manufactured with a protective metal box. Do not use a ballast if any of the wiring or components are not contained within this outer shell. In addition, do not place the ballast within another box. The heat build-up could potentially cause a fire. Ballasts are hot, generally operating between 90-150 degrees. To check if your ballast is running too hot, touch a kitchen safety match on the side of the outer box. If the match lights, your box is too "hot"; have it checked.

 **Rule of Thumb:** During cool months, use the heat from the ballast to heat the garden room. Move the hot ballast outside to cool the garden room when necessary.

Most ballasts are "single tap" and set up for either 120-volt power or 220-volt service (240 volts in Australia). Some ballasts are "multi tap" or "quad tap" and, with internal wiring changes, can be made to operate at 120, 208, 240 or 277 volts. Unless you already have several lamps connected to 220-volt circuit, it is easiest to use the 120-volt system. To

*If a "Strike Anywhere" match ignites when placed on a ballast box, the box is too hot. Take the ballast into the retailer and have it checked out.*

change a ballast from 120 to 220 volts, employ a qualified electrician to move an internal wire from the 120-volt lead to the 220 (208)-volt lead and to change the plug to a 220-volt.

A 220-volt ballast will draw the same watts, but only half the amperes. Wiring several systems for 220 volts as a 110-volt ballast, allows more units to be placed on a breaker circuit. Changing the wiring from 120 to 220 does not save electricity. This is demonstrated by:

Ohm's Power Law:
Watts = volts x amperes

For safety and to ensure the efficiency of your ballast, build a small shelf and place your ballast off the floor and away from any potentially wet areas. Buying a ballast with a handle will ease your work. Ballasts can weigh between 30 and 55 pounds and are awkward to move without a handle. If the ballast creates too much heat for your garden room, use a cooling fan or an air vent. If necessary, you can place your ballast outside of your garden room. However, during cooler months, the ballast can add needed heat to the garden room. (see Appendix C: Troubleshooting HIS Systems).

 **Rule of Thumb:** It takes the same amount of electricity to run a transformer on 110 or 220 volt current.

Before beginning our comparisons of different members of the HID family, we need to review several key terms and concepts. When an efficiency rate is given in lumens-per-watt input, we are referring the lamps efficiency for converting electricity into light which is visible to the human eye. Remember, although plants and humans use an overlapping section of the energy spectrum, the region of light we use is different from that which the plant uses. In making lamp comparisons, you should also consider life-span (how long the bulb will last given a certain amount of daily use) and spectral emission. A lamp that efficiently and inexpensively produces light primarily in the blue and red regions of the spectrum is a wise investment for your garden room because plants use and must have these colors. It is also useful to know how much light coverage a particular lighting system provides. You will find easy-to-use charts throughout this chapter that will help you make comparisons and select a lighting system that will make the most of your investment.

## Mercury Vapor Lamps

Mercury vapor lamps are the grandparents of the HID family. In fact, the concept of HID lights was first applied to mercury vapor lamps at the beginning of the twentieth century. The lamps work by arcing electricity through mercury vapor. Argon gas is used for starting the light.

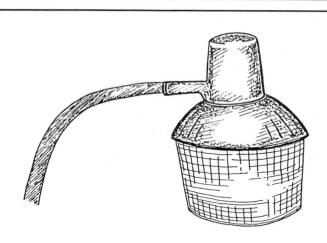

*Old street light fixtures are a big gamble to use.*

Old HID street lights are sometimes found at surplus stores and salvage yards. These old mercury vapor, metal halide and HP sodiums can be a bargain, but only on the surface. These heavy 60 to 70 pound systems are old and tired. A new capacitor and bulb are normally necessary just to start and run them efficiently. The street light reflector is made to function at 40 feet or more. When you aim this reflector and hang it a foot or two above plants, it cooks them. We recommend that you stay away from these dangerous old dinosaurs.

Although they are more efficient than incandescents, tungsten halogen and fluorescent lamps, mercury vapor lamps possess the least efficient lumen-per-watt ratio of any member of the HID family. Mercury vapor lamps produce only 60 lumens-per-watt, less than half of what its closest competitor in efficiency (the metal halide) produces. This low efficiency rate, combined with improper color spectrum makes the mercury vapor lamp a poor choice for horticultural use. Mercury vapor bulbs produce virtually all of their light in the blue region of the spectrum and emit very little of the red light which is also required for photosynthesis. In addition, mercury vapor lamps are expensive to operate because their lumen-per-watt conversion is so low.

Mercury vapor lamps do have some positive attributes. They come in a range of sizes, from 40 to 1000 watts, have fairly good lumen maintenance and a relatively long life. Although there are some slight variations, most wattages last up to three years at18-hours a day of operation. Although most mercury vapor bulbs require separate ballasts, there are several which possess self-contained ballasts. These bulbs (often 250 watts) simply screw into a standard household medium base fixture, just like an incandescent. The disadvantage of this particular mercury vapor bulb is that it is even less efficient than other mercury vapor bulbs and is quite expensive (often in the neighborhood of $100). For a non self-ballasted bulb, remember to buy a compatible ballast; trying to save money on a ballast is usually an expensive experiment.

Mercury vapor lamps can produce fair results in your garden, but they offer no competition to other members of. the HID family. Mercury vapor bulbs produce results equivalent to a cool white fluorescent. With low efficiency, improper color spectrum and the promise of a high electric bill, mercury vapor lamps offer little to the indoor gardener.

## Metal Halide Lamps

There is virtually no comparison between mercury vapor and metal halide lamps. Whereas mercury vapor lamps are essentially obsolete for horticultural purposes, metal halides are popularly used. Many gardeners recommend metal halide lamps above all others. The metal halide lamp produces between 65-115 lumens-per-watt. Perhaps the best defining characteristic of the metal halide is its

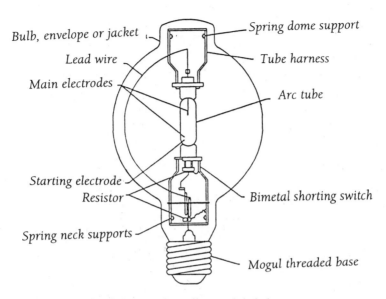

Bulb, envelope or jacket

Lead wire

Main electrodes

Spring dome support

Tube harness

Arc tube

Starting electrode

Resistor

Spring neck supports

Bimetal shorting switch

Mogul threaded base

*This super metal halide lamp has all parts labeled*

excellent spectral distribution. Metal halides emulate bright
summer sunlight and contain all the energy peaks at wavelengths of the visible spectrum. Because these lamps emit
light in the red (600-700 nm), blue (400-500 nm) and far-
red (700-800 nm) regions they are used for horticultural
uses. Metal halides have a high lumen-per-watt conversion
that allows them to foster photosynthesis and other plant
activities that require bright light.

In addition, metal halides have good lumen maintenance and long life expectancy. Having good lumen maintenance means that as the lamp ages, its decline in lumen output is very gradual. A 1000-watt super metal halide lamp
can last up to 12,000 hours or more, which equates to about
two years of 18 hours a day of use. After 12 months of use
at 18 hours per day (6500 hours) most 1000-watt metal
halide lamps should be replaced. At this point a bulb is
about 85 percent as bright as the day you bought it. The

average life of a 400-watt super metal halide is 20,000 hours
and should be replaced after about 10,000 hours or 18
months of 18-hour per day operation.   See Light Bulb Chart
for specific recommendations.  When the lamp fails to start
or fails to reach its full light capacity, you know it has
reached the end of its life.  Metal halides stop performing for
a variety of reasons: lamp electrodes deteriorate, transmis-
sion within the arc tube stops due to blackening, or the
chemical balance within the arc tube shifts.  (If the inner arc
tube is blackened, change it).  The capacitor commonly
causes the lamp to dim or fail.  The capacitor retains an electrical charge to help ignite the lamp.  As the ballast is used,
the capacitor begins to lose its ability to retain the charge.
This translates into a dim lamp.  Some gardeners replace
their capacitors every 2-4 years.  Some capacitors are defec-
tive from the start.  (see Appendix C: Troubleshooting the
HID ) Change the lamp well before it dies.  Old bulbs are
neither cost effective nor efficient.

**Rule of Thumb**: Replace 1000-watt super halide
bulbs after using for 10-12 months at 18-hour days.
Replace most HP sodium bulbs after using 24
months at 12-hour days for optimum performance.
See Light Bulb Chart for specific recommendations.

**Rule of Thumb**: Replace 400-watt super halide bulbs
after using 18 months of 18-hour days.  See Light
Bulb Chart for specific recommendations.

To maximize efficiency, use a timer and only turn
your light on once a day.  A large amount of voltage is
required for the initial ionization process each time the lamp
is started; but this only occurs for a second or less, so does
not add to expense.  The more you turn your lamp on and
off, the faster your bulb will deteriorate.  If you do turn your
light off or if a power surge occurs and shuts the light off, it
will take up to 15 minutes for the lamp to restart.  The arc

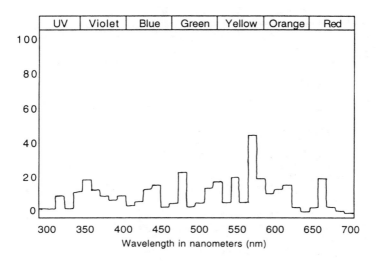

*This spectral analysis graph of a metal halide shows light colors.*

tube gases and the ballast must cool before restarting. (Lamps connected to timers will restart automatically once they cool).

To further maximize efficiency, operate vertical lamps in a vertical position (plus or minus fifteen degrees). Horizontal bulbs (plus or minus 15 degrees of horizontal) and universal bulbs can be operated in any position, 360 degrees. In other positions than vertical a universal bulb will produce lower wattage, lumen output and life expectancy will decrease. This causes premature burnout. HOR or horizontal bulbs require special lamp sockets to keep the arc tube properly oriented. These sockets are designated either POM (Position Oriented Mogul) or POMB (Position Oriented Mobul Base).

Note: Universal bulbs can be operated in any orientation 360 degrees, but they are most efficient in the vertical position. The Light Bulb Chart shows the "Initial Lumens", "Mean Lumens" and the Lumen-per-watts" of both vertical

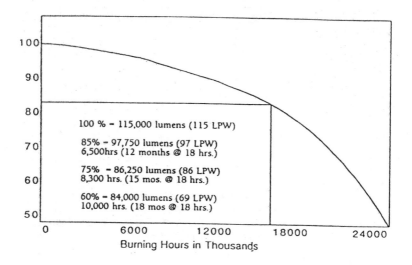

100 %  – 115,000 lumens (115 LPW)

85% – 97,750 lumens (97 LPW)
6,500hrs (12 months @ 18 hrs.)

75% – 86,250 lumens (86 LPW)
8,300 hrs. (15 mos. @ 18 hrs.)

60% – 84,000 lumens (69 LPW)
10,000 hrs. (18 mos @ 18 hrs.)

Burning Hours in Thousands

*Lumen Maintenance Curve for MH Lamps*

and horizontal burning positions for universal bulbs.  Notice that the bulb produces many fewer lumens in the horizontal position.

Metal halide lamps create light by passing electricity through an inner clear arc tube which is enclosed within the vacuum of the outer bulb.  The inner arc tube contains mercury and other metals in iodide form.  The combination of these metals gives the metal halide its spectral advantage over other lamp options.  The outer casing can be either clear or phosphor coated.  Phosphor coated varieties enhance the red part of the spectrum of the lamps giving the bulbs a warmer color and more UV blocking ability.   This also helps to diffuse the light.  Most horticulturists prefer the clear bulb because it provides the brightest white light possible.  Gardeners who use the phosphor coated bulbs like them because they are easier on the eyes;  they emit more diffused light with less ultraviolet rays.  The outer bulb or envelope is glass, which blocks ultraviolet light and lumens.

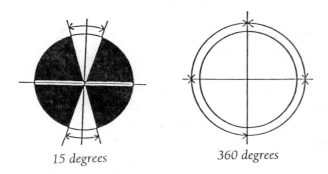

15 degrees                          360 degrees

*Vertical bulbs are designed to operate +- 15 degrees of vertical.*
*Universal bulbs can burn in any position (360 degrees) but are most*
*efficient when vertical.*

Because the metal halide arc system is so complex, it
will take up to 100 hours of use before all the components
stabilize.  During the stabilization period, the lamp may emit
varying colors.  After about 100 hours of operation, the lamp
will emit clear white light, but it will still take several minutes to warm up and begin emitting the characteristic white
light.  In addition, your lamp may pulsate between bright
and dim light.  This stroboscopic effect is a by-product of the
fact that the arc is extinguished 120 times per second.  But
the gases inside the arc tube glow evenly due to self-excita-
tion and, after a few minutes, will not flicker.  It is a normal
aspect of metal halides and will not affect your garden
adversely.

Metal halide bulbs are available in watts ranging from
70 to 1500.  Most gardeners choose either the 250, 400, 600
or the 1000 watt system, depending on the size of their garden room.  Osram/Sylvania, General Electric,
Phillips/Westinghouse, Iwasaki and Venture Lighting all
manufacture metal halide bulbs marketed under various
trade names.  Some gardeners use only the more expensive

and difficult-to-find Iwasaki bulbs, sighting their color spectrum and dependability as superior to others.

 **Rule of Thumb:** Always buy the "Super" version of metal halide bulbs.

Manufacturers also produce "super" versions of most halide bulbs. Although super or high output halides cost slightly more, they are worth the extra investment because of their increased efficiency and output. Super halides emit about 10 percent more lumens than their standard counterparts. Remember, when you are investing in a lighting system, you must consider the return on your money over the long run. If you only consider the initial financial output, you will not maximize your growing dollars. For example, a 400 watt super bulb uses the exact same amount of electricity as a 400 watt standard metal halide. Look for super halides under the trade names Super Metalarc (Osram/Sylvania), High-Output Multivapor (GE), Super Metal Halide (Phillips/Westinghouse), Multi-Metal (Iwasaki) and Super Pro-Arc (Venture).

Three types of metal halide lamps are available: universal (U), vertical (BU or BD) and horizontal (HOR) and most of these lamps are available in clear and phosphor-coated versions. Remember that universal bulbs are less efficient when burned in a non-vertical position. HOR bulbs require a special POMB or POM socket. When purchasing metal halide lamps, check the bulb to make sure there is no flawed glass and check for bent internal components or lose wires. A small sprinkling of glass chips in the bulb causes no trouble, but large bits of glass are unacceptable. For more information and to make comparisons in price, talk to reputable supplier in your area or contact the manufacturers directly.

Both super and standard halide lamps require ballasts. Purchase your lighting system as a complete unit or system so you are assured that the ballast and lamp are com-

patible.  Match your ballast to your lamp according to
wattage.  A 400-watt ballast will operate a 400-watt bulb
regardless of whether it is clear or phosphor coated, standard, or super sized.  You need a different ballast for a 1000-
watt metal halide bulb.  It too will operate all 1000-watt
metal halide bulbs: standard or super, clear or phosphor
coated.

   You must also consider the socket required for the
lamp you choose.  4KV pulse rated mogul socket is required
for metal halide, HP sodium and conversion lamps (150, 175,
250, 360, 400, 430, 600, 940, except for the 1000-watt HPS
which requires a 5KV pulse rated socket.  4KV pulse rated
mogul sockets are generally white or yellow and the 5KV
socket is usually gray.  Horizontal metal halide bulbs may
require a special version of the 4KV pulse rated socket
known as POM or POMB.  If you use the wrong socket, the
lamp may not light or worse yet, it will turn into a potential
fire hazard!  The socket heats and cools with use.  If cracks
develop in the socket, replace it immediately!

   Some gardeners have dubbed metal halides the best
single light available for indoor use.  Although supplemental
light may be necessary if you are trying to induce flowering,
metal halides are an excellent choice for general garden use
and especially for the vegetative growth.

   While some plant varieties will respond to the light
of a HP sodium and grow well, most plants will respond and
grow well with the metal halide's light.  There is so little
information now about the specific varieties that will
respond to HP sodium light that you have to experemient
with diffrent varieties of plants to find out which ones grow
best with only HP sodium light.

   Many gardeners choose to combine metal halides
and HP sodium lamps.  They use a ratio of one metal halide
and two or three HP sodiums.  They use this combination to
promote vegetative growth and then they switch to all sodiums to promote flowering.  There is more on this subject of

color-corrected HP sodium lamps that some gardeners use exclusevieiy for plant growth in the HP sodium section.

For more information on specific bulbs please see the Light Bulb Chart. Bulbs that are listed in bold type are the best value for indoor gardening.

Note: If a metal halide lamp has a scratch on its outer surface, handle it with care. Scratches to the outer surfaces or extreme pressure can cause the bulb to break. Metal halide lamps when they are in use develop ultraviolet radiation. If the outer container of the bulb breaks, be certain to turn the power off immediately to prevent ultraviolet radiation exposure. Do not try to dispose of the lamp until it has completely cooled. Touching or even looking at a shattered, hot metal halide lamp can burn your skin and eyes. Look for instructions with your lamp to familiarize yourself with precautions, operating instructions and disposal procedures.

## High Pressure Sodium Lamps

High pressure (HP) sodium lamps are by far the greatest competitor of metal halides. In fact, gardeners debate which of these two lamps is preferable for general indoor horticultural use. Where the metal halide is weakest, the HP sodium is strongest and vice versa. Although it has a good spectral distribution, the HP sodium can not compare to the metal halide in the blue end of the color spectrum. Sodiums emit light energy concentrated in the yellow and red regions of the spectrum and are weak in the blue-violet end. Because of the limited spectral distribution, some varieties of plants grown with sodium lights alone can become elongated and leggy, while others show little or no effect.

The high cost-efficiency of sodium bulbs, however, offers a great advantage and make them a viable competitor to the metal halide. A metal halide system typically costs 15 to 20 percent less to set up and the replacement bulbs are

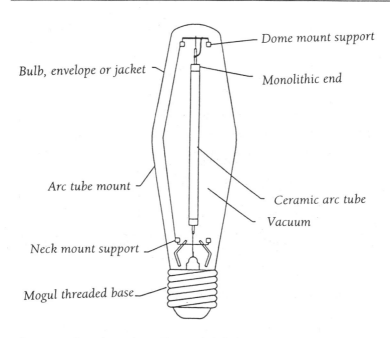

*Bulb, envelope or jacket*

*Dome mount support*

*Monolithic end*

*Arc tube mount*

*Ceramic arc tube*

*Vacuum*

*Neck mount support*

*Mogul threaded base*

*This HP sodium lamp has all parts labeled.*

less expensive than sodiums.  However, sodium bulbs have a longer life span and higher lumen maintenance.  In fact, HP sodiums have a longer life expectancy (up to 24,000 hours) than all other high intensity discharge lamps.  We still recommend changing HPS lamps every 24-27 months.  As your HP sodium bulb nears the end of its life, its chemical balance begins to change.  The sodium seeps out of the arc tube, consequently changing the ratio of mercury to sodium in the tube.  As the chemical balance changes, the voltage in the arc tube rises, eventually to a level which the ballast is not able to sustain.  You will know when your lamp has reached this point because it will shut off after warming up to its full intensity.  Remember, regardless of the lamp you select, all HIDs must be replaced long before the end of their rated life for best results.

High pressure sodium lamps are the brightest lights on the market and lose their intensity more gradually than

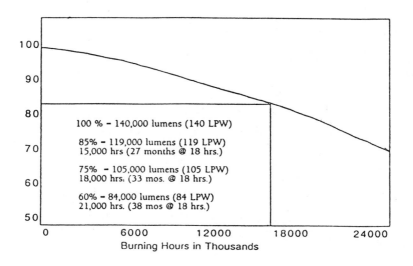

*Approximate lumen maintenance curve for HP sodium lamps.*

do metal halides. Whereas some metal halides lose 15-20 percent of their intensity after one year of use, sodium bulbs lose only5 percent during their first year. In addition, high pressure sodium lamps have a higher lumen-per-watt efficiency than do metal halides. For example, metal halide lamps have a lumen-per-watt conversion of 70 to 115, whileHP sodiums have a lumen-per-watt conversion of 97 to 150. (See Life Expectancy Curve charts of metal halide and HP sodium lamps.)

HP sodiums are more efficient but they are not necessarily a better investment than metal halides for all gardeners. HP sodiums are more expensive and may have a more limited application for the specific varieties you are growing. The fact that high pressure sodium lamps do not have a completely balanced spectral distribution has been their main disadvantage to indoor hobby gardeners. Because their light is weak in the blue region, they are not as well suited for high irradiance required for photosynthesis. If you garden in a greenhouse and can rely on the sun to provide light

in the blue end of the spectrum, HP sodiums are an excellent, highly efficient and highly cost effective choice.
Greenhouse growers worldwide use HP sodium lights to aug-
ment natural sunlight in fruit, vegetable and flower production.  However, if you garden in a basement, garage, spare
room or closet, you must rely entirely on artificial light.  In
such circumstance, HP sodiums might not be used exclusively because of their deficiency in blue light.

Many gardeners have been able to reap the benefits
of high pressure sodiums by using them in combination with
metal halides.  The halides provide the blue light while the
HP sodiums provide additional red light to stimulate flower
and fruit production.  Blue light is necessary, but a small
amount of blue light goes a long way.  Some gardeners recommend a ration of one halide to three or even four sodiums.  We recommend that you experemient with HP sodium
light.  If plants stretch when using only a HP sodim light,
add more blue light with a metal halide.  You may also want
to try the color corrected HP sodium bulbs such as the SON
AGRO or the PLANTA.  A complete discussion on these
bulbs can be found later in this chapter.

The HP sodium bulb is made of a translucent ceramic arc tube  containing sodium, mercury and xenon gas.
This arc tube is contained within an outer glass bulb which
can be either clear or coated.  The clear bulb allows for good
optical clarity and intensity while the coated bulb serves to
diffuse light.  You will find high pressure sodium bulbs ranging from 35-1000 watts.  The 400 and 1000-watt bulbs are
available only in clear, not phosphor coated.  Phosphor-coated HPS lamps are uncommon because the coating changes
the light spectrum very little and they radiate less light.  The
1000-watt bulb is very bright and especially useful for large
spaces and high-intensity plants that require high light intensity.  The 1000-watt bulbs emits an impressive 140,000 initial
lumens.  The 600-watt HPS produces 90,000 initial lumens
and a lumen-per-watt conversion of 150 to make it the most
efficient member of the HID family.

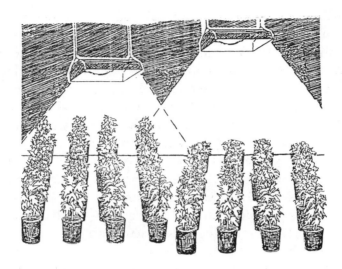

*One of these two plants has been growing under an old HPS with only 60% of its initial lumens and another that grows under a HPS with 90% of its lumens.*

Like other high intensity discharge lamps, HP sodium lights require separate ballasts. Remember to buy a ballast that is compatible with your lamp. Specific ballasts are needed for 400*, 600 and the 1000-watt high pressure sodium lamps. *Note: the 430 watt HPS bulb requires a specific 430 watt HPS ballast. The 1000-watt HPS also requires a 5KV pulse rated socket. Remember, it is generally safest (and ultimately the most time and cost effective) to purchase an entire HID system as opposed to separate components.

HP Sodium bulbs are manufactured under the trade names Lucalox (General Electric), Sunlux or Ignitron (Iwasaki), Lumalux (Osram/Sylvania) and Ceramalux (Phillips/Westinghouse). Two manufacturers market high pressure sodium bulbs which have been color corrected to provide about 6% more blue light in their spectrum including the 430-watt Son Agro (Philips), 600-watt PLANTA

(Osram/Sylvania). If you examine the spectral emission graph of a typical sodium bulb you will find that the total emission in the blue end of the spectrum (400-500 nm) is much less than the green (500-600 nm) or the red (600-700 nm). In fact the blue emission as a percentage of the total emissions is less than 10 percent.

General Electric's Deluxe Lucalox has substantially better color rendition than their Standard Lucalox. Similarly, HP sodium bulbs produced by Iwasaki emit more blue light than average. The most popular color corrected HP sodium bulb is probably the SON AGRO manufactured by Phillips/Westinghouse.

SON AGRO and the SON-T-AGRO (the T signifies tubular bulb) lamps, are also a good choice for gardeners who are concerned about providing sufficient blue light and using only one efficient HP sodium bulb.

According to the manufacturer, the 430-watt SON AGRO produces 30 percent more blue light than standard HP sodiums. They also emit 6 percent more light as a standard 400-watt HP sodium.

The 430-watt HP sodium must have a specific ballast containing a transformer, capacitor and starter. The market for 430-watt HP sodium bulbs has been dominated by professional and hobby growers. In the beginning the market was so small that making 430-watt ballasts was not economical. The transformers for the 400-watt bulbs were substituted and a larger capacitor (56 microfard rather than the standard 55 microfard) was used. As the market grew for the 430-watt bulb, a specific 430-watt transformer and specific capacitor were developed and marketed.

The transformer for a 400-watt HP sodium bulb does not provide the proper range of voltage regulation to make the 430-watt HP sodium bulb function at designed efficiency. This ballast, when used to drive a 430-watt HP sodium lamp will not adhere to **ANSI (?????)** specifications and the lamp will not burn as long nor as brightly. If you use a trans-

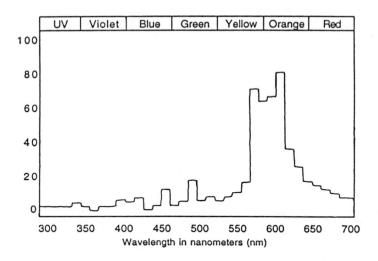

*Color spectrum chart a HP sodium lamp.*

former designed for a 400-watt HP sodium bulb to drive a
430-watt HP sodium bulb, you do not get maximum light for
the electricity invested.

Changing the capacitor gives more output but the
transformer output (a function of line voltage) fluctuates too
much to drive the bulb efficiently.

The 1075-watt HP sodium lamp is very similar to the
430-watt HP sodium with more wattage. The 1075-watt HP
sodium uses a transformer designed for the 1000-watt HP
sodium and a hotter capacitor: 32 microfarads rather than a
26 microfarad capacitor designed for the 1000-watt HP sodium bulb.

The voltage at standard home electrical outlets normally fluctuates from 108 volts to 132 volts. A 108-volt reading is most common when there is a major draw on power
by customers; for example, on a hot day when everybody is
using air conditioning and all the businesses are using electricity at full capacity. A 132-volt reading might occur at
night when few households are using electricity and busi-

nesses are closed. This would be the best time to use electricity in order to get the absolute best efficiency from your transformer, capacitor and bulb.

Checking voltage at the electrical outlet is as simple as using a voltmeter. Try using a voltmeter to check the voltage on different electrical outlets at different times during the day. You may be surprised at your findings! If the voltage is much different between outlets, check the electrical connections.

If you have much deviation in voltage output, employ a qualified eledtrician to troubleshoot the outlets and make sure the highest voltage is supplied.

## Conversion Bulbs

If you already own an HID lighting system and are convinced that a different type of lamp would better suit your needs, do not worry. Conversion or retrofit bulbs allow gardeners increased flexibility. One type of conversion bulb allows you to utilize a metal halide (or mercury vapor) system with a bulb that emits light similar to an HP sodium bulb. The bulb looks like a blend between a metal halide and an HP sodium. While the outer bulb looks like a metal halide, the inner arc tube is similar to that of a HP sodium. A small ignitor is located at the base of the bulb. Other conversion bulbs retrofit HP sodium systems to convert them into a virtual metal halide system.

Conversion bulbs are manufactured in 150, 215, 360, 400, 880, 940 and 1000-watt sizes. You do not need an adapter or any additional equipment. Simply screw the bulb into a compatible ballast of comparable wattage. Conversion bulbs operate at a lower wattage and are not as bright as HP sodium bulbs. Although conversion bulbs have less blue, they are up to 25 percent brighter than metal halide systems and their lumen-per-watt conversion is better than that of

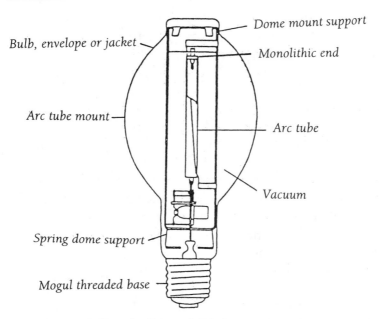

Bulb, envelope or jacket

Dome mount support

Monolithic end

Arc tube mount

Arc tube

Vacuum

Spring dome support

Mogul threaded base

*A conversion bulb with all parts labeled.*

super metal halides. The 940-watt conversion bulb has a lumen-per-watt rating of 138. Similar to the HP sodium lamp, the conversion bulb has a life expectancy of up to 24,000 hours. Unlike most high pressure sodium lamps which flicker on and off near the end of their lives, conversion bulbs go off and remain off at the end of their lives.

Although conversion bulbs are not inexpensive, they are certainly less expensive than an entire HP sodium system. For gardeners who own a metal halide system, or who deem metal halide the most appropriate investment for their lighting needs, conversion bulbs offer a welcome alternative for bright light. C.E.W. Lighting distributes Iwasaki lights in the United States. Look for their Sunlux Super Ace and Sunlux Ultra Ace lamp.

Venture, Iwasaki and Sunlight Supply manufacture bulbs for conversion in the opposite direction, from high pressure sodium to metal halide. Venture's White-Lux and

Iwasaki's White Ace are metal halide lamps which will operate in a HP sodium system. The 250, 400, 1000-watt conversion bulbs can be used in compatible HPS systems with no alterations or additional equipment. 1000 retrofit from Sunlight Supply. If you own a high pressure sodium system, but need the added blue light which metal halide bulbs produce, these conversion bulbs will suit your needs.

Many gardeners have great success using conversion bulbs. If you have a metal halide system, but want the extra red and yellow light of an HP sodium to promote flowering, simply buy a conversion bulb. Instead of investing in both a metal halide and an HP sodium system, you can rely on a metal halide system and use conversion bulbs when necessary, or vice versa. The disadvantage of conversion bulbs is that they you lose some efficiency through the conversion process.

## Low Pressure Sodium Lamps

Low pressure sodium lamps do not compare to high pressure sodiums, metal halide or conversion bulbs when it comes to growing plants. LP sodiums produce light even more heavily based in the yellow and red regions of the spectrum. We do not recommend using low pressure sodium lamps for plant growth. For a complete discussion of low pressure sodium lamps see *The New Revised Gardening Indoors* by George F. Van Patten.

## Sulfur Bulbs

Fusion Lighting has developed an efficient lamp using a benign sulfur. The technology for the bulb is still being researched and is likely to continue to improve in the future. Currently, Fusion Lighting bulbs produce balanced light which maintains its spectral distribution throughout its life.  Unlike most other bulbs on the market, sulfur bulbs produce light in both the red and blue regions.  The bulb has a 95 percent lumen maintenance rating.  It is rated for 10,000 hours of use, although research is being conducted to try to increase the bulb's life expectancy to 20,000 hours. Unlike most HID bulbs, frequent stops and starts do not seem to deteriorate the lifespan of sulfur bulbs.  The bulb's high lumen maintenance and life expectancy are products of its simple design.  The sulfur bulb does not rely on chemical reactions.

If Fusion Light has continued success with their research and are able to offer the sulfur bulb at competitive prices, this bulb will be a viable alternative with horticultural applications.  However, the time we are writing this book, winter of 1996, the cost of a sulfur bulb is about $2,000.


## Bulb Maintenance

Selecting appropriate bulbs, taking care of them and replacing them regularly helps you make the most of your lighting investment.

To keep bulbs working well throughout their lives, remember to dust them on a regular basis.  Dust dulls the intensity of artificial light in the same way that clouds dull the sun's intensity.  You do not want to pay for muted light. Taking the time to keep your bulbs clean will help ensure that you are getting the most out of your bulb investment. Some lighting systems come with a glass shield which pro-tects the bulb from dust and water.  These systems are gener-ally U.L. Listed to ensure their safety.  If your lighting unit does not have such a shield, take care not to get hot bulbs wet when you are misting and watering your garden.

Virtually all bulbs, are "efficient" for about half of their rated life.

HIDs have a lumen maintenance curve and will burn for a couple of years. However, they start to decrease in intensity after 10 to 24 months. After 10 to 12 months of use at 18 hours per day (6500 hours) a metal halide lamp should be replaced. After 27 months of use at 12 hours per day (15000 hours), the HPS should be replaced. (See Light Bulb Chart for specific recommendations). Many gardeners prefer to replact their bulbs sooner than we reccomend and say they have the best results with newer bulbs. Following this general rule, you will see consistent growth. If you are growing low light plants and do now care if your garden's growth slows, wait 18 to 24 months to replace bulbs. Light intensity of a 1000 watt super metal halide that burns for 18 hours per day for 12 months will loose 15 percent of its original light output. The same lamp that runs for 18 months at 18 hours per day will loose 40 percent or more of its original light output. (See "Life Expectancy Curves" of Metal Halide Lamps"). Plants will stretch toward the bulb when they do not receive enough intense light.

If you are unable to replace your HID bulb as often as necessary you have an option. The dimmer bulb does not produce as much heat, so you can move it closer to the garden and bunch plants closer together. Remember, light diminishes to the square of the distance. The closer the lamp is to the garden, the brighter the light.

 **Rule of Thumb:** Replace 1000-watt super halide bulbs after using 10-12 months of 18-hour days. Replace most HP sodium bulbs after using 24 months of 12-hour days for optimum performance. See Light Bulb Chart for specific recommendations.

 **Rule of Thumb:** Replace 400-watt super halide bulbs after using 18 months of 18-hour days. See Light Bulb Chart for specific recommendations.

We recommended that you write down the day, month and year you bought the HID so that you can calculate when to replace it for best results. It is virtually impossible to look at the bulb or the light the bulb emits with your naked eye and discern when to change the bulb. Remember the pupils in your eyes open and close to compensate for different light levels.

 **Rule of Thumb:** Use a light meter to measure the foot-candle output of the bulb the week after it is set up. Measure output again each month. Make sure to measure output in the exact same place and at the same distance from the source so that the test will be consistent.

All bulbs deteriorate with time. That is, the light that they emit decreases in intensity as the bulb ages. To make the most of your lighting investment, we advise that you replace lamps long before they burn out. As bulbs near the end of their lives, they loose efficiency and are less cost effective. One way to make an educated guess as to the age or life expectancy of HID bulbs is to look at the inner quartz arc-tube. If it looks really cloudy or is blackened, it is probably time to replace it.

Touching the bulb leaves the oily residue of yoy=ur hands on the bulb. This oil is baked into the bulb and weakens it. Use rubbing alcohol to clean the bulb of all dirt and grime.

If a drop of water touches a hot bulb, it could explode. Be very careful with water in your garden. Do not spray the garden when the bulb is on. Wait for the bulb to cool down before splashing water around.

CAUTION! If the outer shell (envelope) breaks on HID bulbs, they may not go out. Turn off immediately and DO NOT LOOK AT THE ARC TUBE WHEN LIT! Severe eye damage can occur.  Harmful ultraviolet (UV) light is being emitted!  Severe eye damage and skin burn can occur!

Note:  All HID bulbs, including HP sodiums get quite hot during operation and tend to expand in their sockets. Do not remove a high pressure sodium bulb or any HID from its socket when it is hot as it is likely to need forcing which could break the bulb.  If the outer casing of the bulb is broken or scratched, avoid contact with metal parts to prevent electrical shock.  Many manufacturers recommend wearing gloves and safety glasses when handling  HID lamps.

## Lamp Disposal

Regardless of which HID lamp you choose to use, you must use caution when disposing of it.  Remember, these lamps contain materials that are harmful to your skin and your eyes.  Avoid contact with the lamps and wear protective clothing.  Place the lamp in a dry container and put in the trash.  Never place a bulb in a fire.  For further recommendations on bulb disposal, contact the manufacturer.

## HID Bulb Chart

This chart was facinating to compile.  There have been so many new dditions to the HID bulb product lines in the last few years. There is an entire new selection of conversion bulbs and clor enhanced HP sodium bulbs that did not exist a few years ago.  The re are aslo many new bulb shapes that fit in reflective hoods much better.

This chart is based upon information from manufacturers specifications.  Please note that bulbs could deviate as much as 15 percent from these figures.  The chart does not

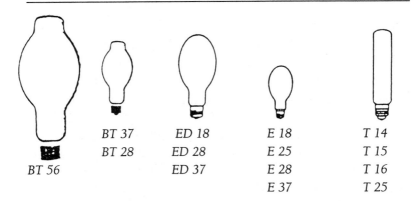

| BT 37 | ED 18 | E 18 | T 14 |
| BT 28 | ED 28 | E 25 | T 15 |
| BT 56 | ED 37 | E 28 | T 16 |
|       |       | E 37 | T 25 |

contain each and every bulb available on the market. Some bulbs on this chart are not available in every country in the world. There are some bulbs that are very common in Europe and Australia that are not aviailble or very difficult to find in North America. The best example is the 600-watt HP sodium PLANRTA bulb. As this book goes to press, we just found out about a new 1000-watt conversion bulb that was just released. We did our absolute best to include all bulbs that indoor gardeners normally use. We would appreciate any updates on bulbs that we should know about.

Entries that are bold faced type are the bulbs that are most often used and recommended by suppliers. These bulbs are the ones that give the most amount of light in the proper spectrum. We feel they are the best values available.

This HID Bulb chart reflects many of the HID bulbs that are available to gardeners today. Bulbs on this chart are rated for (glass) enclosed fixtures. The first column contains the name and type of bulb, the second column is the manufacturer. Bulb shape is listed in column three. Bulbs come intwo basic shapes: bulbous and tubular. The bulbular bulba are given the designation "BT", "ED", "E", and "ET". BT = Blown Tubular, ED = Eliptical Dimple, E = Eliptical. The number refers to the circumference of the bulb in centimeters. Examples include: BT-56, ED-37, E-23.5. Tubular bulbs have the designation: "T". Examples include: T-15, T-

25. The base column notes the type of socket. Finish column designates between C = Clear and P = Phosphor coated. The % less phosphorus column lists the % less lumen output a phosphor coated bulb emitts compared to an identical clear bulb. Burning position is either U = Universal 360 degrees, V = Vertical, BU = Base Up or HOR = Horizontal. Initial lumens is the output of the bulb shortly after the very first use. Mean lumens are figuerd after 100 hours of use. Kelvin temperature defines the color of the light emitted. There is an excellent color kelvin temperature chart on the back cover of this book. The CRI = Color Rendering Index is the accuracy of color rendering. Initial lumens-per-watt (LPW) is the LPW conversion of the bulb. EThe next three columns give you the approximate LPW of each bulb at diffrent hours of rated life. Average hours of life for each bulb is in the next column and the suggested number of hours of use before replacement is given in the last column.

## Key to Abreviations

MH = Metal Halide
MS = Super Metal Halide (about 10% brighter than MH)
HPS = High Pressure Sodium Bulb
HO = High Output

M = Mogul Socket
M1 = POM = Position Oriented Mogul Socket
M1 = POMB = Position Oriented Mogul Base/Socket

C = Clear Bulb
P = Phosphor Coated Bulb
P=??% Phospher Coated Bulb = ??(less)% output than Clear Bulb
N = None
No Stats. = No Statistics Available
H = Horizontal Operate +- 15 degrees of horizontal

BU = Base Up operate +- 15 degrees of vertical
U = 360 degree operation capability
U* = No Statistics available for horizontal burning position
(Universal bulb in horizontal position normally produces 25% fewer lumens)

Degrees Kelvin = Light Color Output
LPW = Lumens per Watt (Initial Lumens divided by watts)
CRI = Color Rendering Index

Mfrg. = Manufacturer
G = General Electric
I = Iwasaki
O = Osram/Sylvania
Ph = Philips/Westinghouse
S = Sunlight Supply
V = Venture

| Lamp | Mfrg | Bulb Shape | Base | Finish | % Less Phosph | Burning Position | Initial Lumens | Mean Lumens | Kelvin Temp. | CRI | Initial LPW | LPW/85% Life-Hrs. | LPW/75% Life-Hrs | LPW/60% Replace | Average Life-Hrs | Replace Life-Hrs |
|---|---|---|---|---|---|---|---|---|---|---|---|---|---|---|---|---|
| **175 Watt Metal Halide** | | | | | | | | | | | | | | | | |
| Multivapor | G | E28 | M | C | P | U V | 14000 | 10350 | 4000 | 65 | 80 | 59 | 52 | 42 | 10000 | 5400 |
| | | | | | | U H | 12000 | 8300 | | 65 | 69 | 49 | 44 | 35 | 6000 | 3240 |
| Multivapor (SP30) | G | E28 | M | P | | U V | 12000 | 8300 | 3000 | 65 | 69 | 49 | 44 | 35 | 10000 | 5400 |
| | | | | | | U H | 10300 | 7100 | | 65 | 59 | 42 | 37 | 30 | 6000 | 3240 |
| **HO Multivapor** | G | E28 | MI | C | P | H | 15000 | 12000 | 4000 | 65 | 86 | 66 | 58 | 46 | 10000 | 5400 |
| Multi-Metal | I | BT28 | M | C | P=4% | U V | 14000 | 11000 | 4200 | 65 | 80 | 61 | 54 | 43 | 10000 | 5400 |
| | | | | | | U H | 12000 | 94000 | | | 69 | 257 | 227 | 182 | | |
| **Super Metalarc** | O | BT28 | MI | C | P=6% | H | 15000 | 12000 | 4400 | 65 | 86 | 66 | 58 | 46 | 7500 | 4050 |
| Super Metalarc 3K | O | BT28 | MI | P | N | H | 13000 | 9500 | 3200 | 70 | 74 | 55 | 48 | 39 | 7500 | 4050 |
| Metal Halide | Ph | ED28 | M | C | P=5% | U* | 13000 | 10350 | 4000 | 65 | 74 | 57 | 50 | 40 | 10000 | 5400 |
| Metal Halide 3K | Ph | ED28 | M | P | N | BU | 12000 | 9000 | 3200 | 70 | 69 | 51 | 45 | 36 | 10000 | 5400 |
| **Super Metal Halide** | Ph | ED28 | MI | C | P=6% | H | 15000 | 12000 | 4300 | 65 | 86 | 66 | 58 | 46 | 10000 | 5400 |
| MH | V | ED28 | M | C | P=7% | U* | 14000 | 10500 | 4000 | 65 | 80 | 60 | 53 | 42 | 10000 | 5400 |
| MH 5K/Daylight | V | ED28 | M | C | N | U* | 12000 | 9000 | 5200 | 75 | 69 | 51 | 45 | 36 | 7500 | 4050 |
| **Super MH** | V | ED28 | MI | C | P=3% | H | 15000 | 11600 | 4000 | 65 | 86 | 65 | 57 | 46 | 10000 | 5400 |
| Super Super MH 3K | V | ED28 | MI | P | N | H | 15000 | 11600 | 4000 | 65 | 86 | 65 | 57 | 46 | 10000 | 5400 |
| **250 Watt Metal Halide** | | | | | | | | | | | | | | | | |
| Multivapor | G | E28 | M | C | P | U V | 21000 | 17000 | 4200 | 65 | 84 | 65 | 57 | 46 | 10000 | 5400 |
| | | | | | | U H | 19500 | 14000 | | | 78 | 57 | 50 | 40 | | |
| Multivapor (SP30) | G | E28 | M | P | | U V | 18000 | 14200 | 3000 | 70 | 72 | 55 | 48 | 39 | 10000 | 5400 |
| | | | | | | U H | 17600 | 13950 | | | 70 | 54 | 47 | 38 | | |
| **HO Multivapor** | G | E28 | MI | C | P | H | 23000 | 18000 | 4200 | 65 | 92 | 70 | 62 | 49 | 10000 | 5400 |

| Lamp | Mfrg | Bulb Shape | Base | Finish | % Less Phosph | Burning Position | Initial Lumens | Mean Lumens | Kelvin Temp. | CRI | Initial LPW | LPW/85% Life-Hrs. | LPW/75% Life-Hrs | LPW/60% Replace | Average Life-Hrs | Replace Life-Hrs |
|---|---|---|---|---|---|---|---|---|---|---|---|---|---|---|---|---|
| *250 Watt Metal Halide* | | | | | | | | | | | | | | | | |
| Multi-Metal | I | BT28 | M | C | P=14% | U V | 21000 | 17000 | 4200 | 65 | 84 | 65 | 57 | 46 | 10000 | 5400 |
| | | | | | | U H | 19500 | 15700 | | | 78 | 60 | 53 | 42 | 10000 | |
| Multi-Metal | I | T16 | M | C | N | H | 18200 | | | | 73 | 31 | 27 | 22 | 9000 | 4860 |
| **Supre Metalarc** | O | BT28 | M1 | C | P=6% | H | 23000 | 18000 | 4200 | 65 | 92 | 70 | 62 | 49 | 10000 | 5400 |
| Super Metalarc 3K | O | BT28 | M1 | P | | H | 21500 | 16500 | 3200 | 70 | 86 | 65 | 57 | 46 | 10000 | 5400 |
| Metal Halide | Ph | ED28 | M | C | P=6% | U* | 20500 | 17000 | 4000 | 65 | 82 | 64 | 56 | 45 | 10000 | 5400 |
| Metal Halide 3K | Ph | ED28 | M | P | N | BU | 18000 | 14200 | 3200 | 70 | 72 | 55 | 48 | 39 | 10000 | 5400 |
| **Super Metal Halide** | Ph | ED28 | M1 | C | P=6% | H | 23000 | 18000 | 4300 | 65 | 92 | 70 | 62 | 49 | 10000 | 5400 |
| MH | V | ED28 | M | C | P=0% | U* | 21000 | 15800 | 4000 | 65 | 84 | 63 | 55 | 44 | 10000 | 5400 |
| MH 5K/Daylight | V | ED28 | M | C | N | U* | 19000 | 14300 | 5200 | 75 | 76 | 57 | 50 | 40 | 7500 | 4050 |
| **Super MH** | V | ED28 | M1 | C | P=2% | H | 23000 | 17300 | 4000 | 65 | 92 | 69 | 60 | 48 | 10000 | 5400 |
| Super MH 3K | V | ED28 | M1 | P | N | H | 21500 | 16200 | 3200 | 70 | 86 | 64 | 57 | 45 | 10000 | 5400 |
| *400 Watt Metal Halide* | | | | | | | | | | | | | | | | |
| Multivapor (SP30) | G | ED28 | M | C | P | U V | 36000 | 28800 | 4000 | 65 | 90 | 69 | 61 | 49 | 20000 | 10800 |
| | | | | | | U H | 15000 | 29800 | | | | 48 | 42 | 34 | | |
| HO Multivapor | G | E37 | M1 | C | P | H | 40000 | 32000 | 4200 | 65 | 100 | 77 | 68 | 54 | 20000 | 10800 |
| HO Multivapor | G | E37 | M | C | P | BU | 40000 | 32000 | 4000 | 65 | 100 | 77 | 68 | 54 | 20000 | 10800 |
| Multi-Metal | I | BT37 | M | C | P | U V | 38000 | 30000 | 4200 | 65 | 95 | 72 | 64 | 51 | 20000 | 10800 |
| | | | | | | U H | 34000 | 26800 | | | 85 | 65 | 57 | 46 | | |
| **Multi-Metal** | I | BT37 | M | C | P | H | 42000 | 30000 | 4200 | 65 | 105 | 77 | 68 | 54 | 20000 | 10800 |
| Multi-Metal | I | T16 | M | C | N | H | 32000 | | | | 80 | 34 | 30 | 24 | 9000 | 4860 |

| Lamp | Mfrg | Bulb Shape | Base | Finish | % Less Phosphe | Burning Position | Initial Lumens | Mean Lumens | Kelvin Temp. | CRI | Initial LPW | LPW/85% Life-Hrs. | LPW/75% Life-Hrs | LPW/60% Replace | Average Life-Hrs | Replace Life-Hrs |
|---|---|---|---|---|---|---|---|---|---|---|---|---|---|---|---|---|
| **400 Watt Metal Halide** | | | | | | | | | | | | | | | | |
| Super Metalarc | O | BT37 | M1 | C | P=3% | H | 40000 | 32000 | 4200 | 65 | 100 | 77 | 68 | 54 | 20000 | 10800 |
| Super Metalarc 3K | O | BT37 | M | P | N | H | 36000 | 27000 | 3200 | 70 | 90 | 67 | 59 | 47 | 20000 | 10800 |
| Metal Halide | Ph | ED28 | M | P | N | U* | 36000 | 28800 | 4000 | 65 | 90 | 69 | 61 | 49 | 12000 | 6480 |
| **Super Metal Halide** | **Ph** | ED37 | M1 | C | P=3% | H | 40000 | 32000 | 4300 | 65 | 100 | 77 | 68 | 54 | 20000 | 10800 |
| MH | V | ED37 | M | C | P=6% | U* | 36000 | 28800 | 4000 | 65 | 90 | 69 | 61 | 49 | 20000 | 10800 |
| MH 5K/Daylight | V | ED37 | M | C | N | U* | 32500 | 26000 | 5200 | 75 | 81 | 62 | 55 | 44 | 15000 | 8100 |
| **Super MH** | **V** | ED37 | M1 | C | P=6% | H | 40000 | 32000 | 4000 | 65 | 100 | 77 | 68 | 54 | 20000 | 10800 |
| **Agro Sun** | **V** | ED37 | M1 | C | N | H | 40000 | 32000 | 3250 | 70 | 100 | 77 | 68 | 54 | 20000 | 10800 |
| Super MH 3K | V | ED37 | M1 | C | N | H | 36000 | 27800 | 3200 | 70 | 90 | 68 | 60 | 48 | 20000 | 10800 |
| **1000 Watt Metal Halide** | | | | | | | | | | | | | | | | |
| AgroSun Multivapor (SP30) | G | BT56 | M | C | N | U V | 110000 | 88000 | 4000 | 65 | 110 | 84 | 74 | 59 | 12000 | 6480 |
| | | | | | | U H | 107800 | 86240 | | | 108 | 82 | 73 | 58 | | |
| HO Multivapor | G | BT56 | M | C | N | BU | 115000 | 92000 | 3800 | 65 | 115 | 88 | 78 | 62 | 12000 | 6480 |
| | | | | | | | | | | | | 0 | 0 | 0 | | |
| **Multi-Metal** | **I** | BT56 | M | C | P | U V | 115000 | 90000 | 4200 | 65 | 115 | 87 | 77 | 62 | 12000 | 6480 |
| | | | | | | U H | 110000 | 86300 | | | | 83 | 74 | 59 | | |
| **Super Metalarc** | **O** | BT56 | M | C | P=4% | BU | 115000 | 92000 | 3600 | 65 | 115 | 88 | 78 | 62 | 12000 | 6480 |
| Metal Halide | Ph | BT37 | M | C | N | U* | 110000 | 88000 | 3700 | 65 | 110 | 84 | 74 | 59 | 10000 | 5400 |

| Lamp | Mfrg | Bulb Shape | Base | Finish | % Less Phosph | Burning Position | Initial Lumens | Mean Lumens | Kelvin Temp. | CRI | Initial LPW | LPW/85% Life-Hrs. | LPW/75% Life-Hrs | LPW/60% Replace | Average Life-Hrs | Replace Life-Hrs |
|---|---|---|---|---|---|---|---|---|---|---|---|---|---|---|---|---|
| **1000 Watt Metal Halide** | | | | | | | | | | | | | | | | |
| MH | V | BT56 | M | C | P=4% | U* | 110000 | 88000 | 4000 | 65 | 110 | 84 | 74 | 59 | 12000 | 6480 |
| MH 5K/Daylight | V | BT56 | M | C | N | U* | 80000 | 64000 | 5200 | 75 | 80 | 61 | 54 | 43 | 9000 | 4860 |
| Super MH | V | BT56 | M | P | P=4% | BU | 115000 | 92000 | 4000 | 65 | 115 | 88 | 78 | 62 | 12000 | 6480 |
| Agro Sun | V | BT37 | M1 | C | N | H | 115000 | 92000 | 3250 | 70 | 115 | 88 | 78 | 62 | 12000 | 6480 |
| Super MH | V | BT37 | M? | C | N | H | 115000 | 92000 | 4000 | 65 | 115 | 88 | 78 | 62 | 12000 | 6480 |
| **150 Watt HP Sodium** | | | | | | | | | | | | | | | | |
| Lucalox | G | E23.5 | M | C | P | U | 16000 | 14400 | 2000 | 22 | 107 | 86 | 76 | 61 | 24000 | 15000 |
| Lucalox | G | E28 | M | C | P | U | 15000 | 13500 | 2000 | 22 | 100 | 81 | 71 | 57 | 24000 | 15000 |
| Lucalox | G | E23.5 | M | C | P | U | 10500 | 9135 | 2200 | 65 | 70 | 56 | 49 | 39 | 15000 | 9375 |
| Sunlux | I | ED28 | M | C | | U | 16000 | 14400 | 2100 | 21 | 107 | 86 | 76 | 61 | 24000 | 15000 |
| Sunlux | I | ED23.5 | M | C | | U | 16000 | 14400 | 2100 | 21 | 107 | 86 | 76 | 61 | 24000 | 15000 |
| Sunlux | I | T15 | M | C | | U | 14500 | 13050 | | | 97 | 78 | 69 | 55 | 24000 | 15000 |
| Ignitron | I | ED23.5 | M | C | | U | 16000 | 14400 | 2100 | 29 | 107 | 86 | 76 | 61 | 24000 | 15000 |
| Lumalux | O | ED23.5 | M | C | P=6% | U | 16000 | 14400 | 2100 | | 107 | 86 | 76 | 61 | 24000 | 15000 |
| Lumalux | O | BT28 | M | C | N | U | 16000 | 14400 | 2100 | | 107 | 86 | 76 | 61 | 24000 | 15000 |
| Lumalux | O | T7 | M | C | N | U | 15000 | 13500 | 2100 | | 100 | 81 | 71 | 57 | 10000 | 6250 |
| Ceramalux | Ph | ED23.5 | M | C | P=6% | U | 16000 | 14400 | 2100 | 21 | 107 | 86 | 76 | 61 | 24000 | 15000 |
| Ceramalux | Ph | ED28 | M | C | N | U | 16000 | 14400 | 2100 | 21 | 107 | 86 | 76 | 61 | 24000 | 15000 |
| **250 Watt HP Sodium HPS** | | | | | | | | | | | | | | | | |
| Lucalox | G | E18 | M | C | N | U | 30000 | 28000 | 2100 | 22 | 120 | 99 | 87 | 70 | 24000 | 15000 |
| Lucalox | G | E18 | M | C | N | U | 22500 | 20700 | 2100 | 65 | 90 | 73 | 65 | 52 | 15000 | 9375 |

| Lamp | Mfrg | Shape | Base | Finish | % Less Phosph | Burning Position | Initial Lumens | Mean Lumens | Kelvin Temp. | CRI | Initial LPW | LPW/85% Life-Hrs. | LPW/75% Life-Hrs. | LPW/60% Replace | Average Life-Hrs | Replace Life-Hrs |
|---|---|---|---|---|---|---|---|---|---|---|---|---|---|---|---|---|
| **250 Watt HP Sodium HPS** | | | | | | | | | | | | | | | | |
| Sunlux | I | ED18 | M | C | P | U | 27500 | 24700 | 2100 | 21 | 110 | 89 | 78 | 63 | 24000 | 15000 |
| Sunlux | I | T15 | M | C | N | U | 29000 | 24750 | | | 116 | 91 | 81 | 65 | 24000 | 15000 |
| **Ignitron** | **I** | **T15** | **M** | **C** | **P** | **U** | **30000** | **27000** | **2100** | **29** | **120** | **97** | **86** | **68** | **24000** | **15000** |
| Lumalux | O | ET18 | M | C | N | U | 29000 | 26100 | | | 116 | 94 | 83 | 66 | 24000 | 15000 |
| Lumalux | O | BT28 | M | P | N | U | 26000 | 23400 | | | 104 | 84 | 74 | 59 | 24000 | 15000 |
| Ceramalux | Ph | ED18 | M | C | N | U | 28500 | 25600 | 2100 | 21 | 114 | 92 | 81 | 65 | 24000 | 15000 |
| Ceramalux | Ph | ED28 | M | P | N | U | 26000 | 24300 | 2100 | 21 | 104 | 86 | 75 | 60 | 24000 | 15000 |
| **400 Watt HP Sodium** | | | | | | | | | | | | | | | | |
| **Lucalox** | **G** | **E18** | **M** | **C** | **N** | **U** | **51000** | **45000** | **2100** | **22** | **128** | **102** | **90** | **72** | **24000** | **15000** |
| Lucalox | G | E37 | M | C | N | U | 47500 | 42750 | 2100 | 22 | 119 | 96 | 85 | 68 | 24000 | 15000 |
| Lucalox | G | E28 | M | C | P | U | 37400 | 34400 | 2200 | 70 | 94 | 76 | 67 | 54 | 15000 | 9375 |
| **Sunlux** | **I** | **ED18** | **M** | **C** | **P** | **U** | **50000** | **45000** | **2100** | **21** | **125** | **101** | **89** | **71** | **24000** | **15000** |
| **Sunlux** | **I** | **T15** | **M** | **C** | | **U** | **50000** | **45000** | | | **125** | **101** | **89** | **71** | **24000** | **15000** |
| **Ignitron** | **I** | **T15** | **M** | **C** | **P** | **U** | **50000** | **45000** | **2100** | **29** | **125** | **101** | **89** | **71** | **24000** | **15000** |
| Lumalux | O | ET18 | M | C | N | U | 50000 | 45000 | | | 125 | 101 | 89 | 71 | 24000 | 15000 |
| Lumalux | O | BT37 | M | P | N | U | 47500 | 42300 | | | 119 | 95 | 84 | 67 | 24000 | 15000 |
| Ceramalux | Ph | ED18 | M | C | N | U | 50000 | 45000 | 2100 | 21 | 125 | 101 | 89 | 71 | 24000 | 15000 |
| Ceramalux | Ph | ED37 | M | P | N | U | 47500 | 42750 | 2100 | 21 | 119 | 96 | 85 | 68 | 24000 | 15000 |

| Lamp | Mfrg | Bulb Shape | Base | Finish | Phospho | % Less Phospho | Burning Position | Initial Lumens | Mean Lumens | Kelvin Temp. | CRI | Initial LPW | LPW/85% Life-Hrs. | LPW/75% Life-Hrs. | LPW/60% Replace | Average Life-Hrs | Replace Life-Hrs |
|---|---|---|---|---|---|---|---|---|---|---|---|---|---|---|---|---|---|
| **430 Watt HP Sodium** | | | | | | | | | | | | | | | | | |
| Son Agro | Ph | ED18 | M | C | | | U | 53000 | 47700 | 2100 | 21 | 123 | 100 | 88 | 70 | 16000 | 10000 |
| Son T Agro | Ph | T | M | C | | | U | | | | | 0 | | | | | |
| Lumalux (PLANTA) | O | | | | | | No special ballast | | | | | | | | | | |
| **600 Watt HP Sodium** | | | | | | | | | | | | | | | | | |
| Lumalux | O | T16 | M | C | N | | U | 90000 | 81000 | 2200 | 25 | 150 | 121 | 107 | 86 | 18000 | 11250 |
| Lumalox (Super) | O | | | | | | | | | | | | | | | | |
| Lumalux (PLANTA) | O | T16 | M | C | N | | U | 81000 | 72900 | | | 135 | 109 | 96 | 77 | 18000 | 11250 |
| Ceramalux | Ph | T14 | M | C | N | | U | 90000 | 81000 | 2100 | 21 | 150 | 121 | 107 | 86 | 18000 | 11250 |
| SON AGRO PLUS | Ph | | | | | | | | | | | | | | | | |
| **1000 Watt HP Sodium** | | | | | | | | | | | | | | | | | |
| Lucalox | G | E25 | M | C | N | | U | 140000 | 12600 | 2100 | 22 | 140 | 65 | 57 | 46 | 24000 | 15000 |
| Sunlux | I | E25 | M | C | | | U | 140000 | 126000 | 2100 | 21 | 140 | 113 | 100 | 80 | 24000 | 15000 |
| Sunlux | I | T25 | M | C | N | | U | 140000 | 126000 | | | 140 | 113 | 100 | 80 | 24000 | 15000 |
| Ignitron | I | T | M | C | N | | U | 140000 | 126000 | 2100 | 25 | 140 | 113 | 100 | 80 | 24000 | 15000 |
| Lumalux | O | E25 | M | C | | | U | 140000 | 126000 | | | 140 | 113 | 100 | 80 | 24000 | 15000 |
| Ceramalux | Ph | ED37 | M | C | | | U | 135000 | 122000 | 2100 | 21 | 135 | 109 | 96 | 77 | 24000 | 15000 |
| Ceramalux | Ph | E25 | M | C | | | U | 140000 | 126000 | 2100 | 21 | 140 | 113 | 100 | 80 | 24000 | 15000 |

| Lamp | Mfrg | Bulb Shape | Base | Finish | % Less Phosph | Burning Position | Initial Lumens | Mean Lumens | Kelvin Temp. | CRI | Initial LPW | LPW/85% Life-Hrs. | LPW/75% Life-Hrs | LPW/60% Replace | Average Life-Hrs | Replace Life-Hrs |
|---|---|---|---|---|---|---|---|---|---|---|---|---|---|---|---|---|
| **250 Watt HPS to MH Conversion (Retrofit) Bulbs** | | | | | | | | | | | | | | | | |
| White Ace | I | ED37 | M | C | P=0% | U | 16000 | 11600 | | | 64 | 47 | 41 | 33 | 10000 | 5400 |
| Retrolux (215 watt) | Ph | ED28 | M | C | | U | 23000 | 10700 | 1900 | 25 | 92 | 57 | 51 | 40 | 2400 | 1296 |
| White Lux | V | ED28 | M | C | P=4% | BU | 18000 | 13500 | 4000 | 65 | 72 | 54 | 47 | 38 | | |
| **400 Watt HPS to MH Conversion (Retrofit) Bulbs** | | | | | | | | | | | | | | | | |
| White Ace | I | ED28 | M | C | P=0% | U | 36000 | 28800 | 4000 | 65 | 90 | 69 | 61 | 49 | 20000 | 10800 |
| White Lux | V | ED28 | M | C | P=4% | BU | 40000 | 3000 | 4000 | 65 | 100 | 46 | 40 | 32 | 20000 | 10800 |
| **1000 Watt HPS to MH Conversion (Retrofit) Bulbs** | | | | | | | | | | | | | | | | |
| Retro-Lux | S | | M | C | | U | 110000 | | 4000 | 65 | 110 | 47 | 41 | 33 | 12000 | |
| White Lux | I | | M | | | U | | | | | | 0 | 0 | 0 | | |
| **360 Watt Conversion Bulbs - Converts 400 Watt MH to 360 Watt HPS** | | | | | | | | | | | | | | | | |
| Sunlux Super Ace | I | BT37 | M | C | P=4% | U | 45000 | 40500 | 2100 | 25 | 125 | 101 | 89 | 71 | 24000 | 12960 |
| Sunlux Ultra Ace | I | BT37 | M | C | P=4% | U | 45000 | 40500 | 2100 | 25 | 125 | 101 | 89 | 71 | 24000 | 12960 |
| Retrolux | Ph | ED37 | M | C | | U | 45000 | 40500 | 1900 | 25 | 125 | 101 | 89 | 71 | 24000 | 12960 |
| **940 Watt Conversion Bulbs - Converts 1000 Watt MH to 940 Watt HPS** | | | | | | | | | | | | | | | | |
| Sunlux Super Ace | I | BT56 | M | C | P=5% | U | 130000 | 117000 | 2000 | 25 | 138 | 112 | 99 | 79 | 24000 | 12960 |
| Sunlux Ultra Ace | I | BT56 | M | C | P=5% | U | 130000 | 117000 | 21000 | 25 | 138 | 112 | 99 | 79 | 24000 | 12960 |

# Chapter Four:
# Getting the Most From Your
# Light Investment

## Light Reflectors

There are several drawbacks you must consider when growing with artificial light. The more aware you are of the drawbacks, the more you can work to correct them and increase light output. Artificial light decreases in intensity as you move away from its source. Artificial light doesn't just fade, it fades fast. Using the proper light reflector can increase the amount of light by up to forty percent. Because artificial light fades as it travels from its source (the bulb), the closer you put the reflector to the bulb, the more intense the light it reflects will be.

We recommend that you purchase a prefabricated reflector rather than trying to make your own. Manufactured reflectors are hoods that surround a portion of the lamp to direct light toward plants. Although they are more expensive, some gardeners prefer enclosed hoods which are made with glass shields. The shield covers the bulb and keeps water from causing damage to your lamp. In addition, these glass shields serve as a barrier between plants and the heat of the bulb. If you opt for a hood with a glass shield, it is imperative that it has a vent. Otherwise, the glass will trap heat near the bulb and could cause premature burnout.

Reflective hoods are generally made of steel sheet metal or aluminum. The steel is either cold rolled or pre-galvanized before a reflective coating is applied. We recommend pre-galvanized steel which is more rust resistant than cold rolled steel. The reflective coating on most steel hoods and some aluminum hoods is white. The premium ones apply white paint in a powder coating process. Aluminum reflective hoods can also be painted white or powder coated white. Textured aluminum reflective hoods are popular. The various types of textured surfaces (specular (mirror), semi-specular (dull mirror), pebble tone (fine dimples), hammer tone (large dimples)) offer good diffusion and more surface area for the reflective light. Watch for hot spots when purchasing highly reflective polished, mirror-like aluminum. It can also smudge and scratch easily.

When purchasing a reflective hood, consider its size, reflective capabilities and application. Look for a reflector that does not reflect light back into its own walls.

Horizontal reflectors are the most effective and offer the best all round value. Hanging a lamp horizontally increases light output greatly. In the book *New Revised Gardening Indoors*, Van Patten, proved that a horizontal reflector emitted at least 40 percent more light than a vertical cone shaped reflector. As the light is emitted from the arc tube, half of it is directed downward to the plants. The other half can easily be directed toward plants with a reflector. Horizontal reflective hoods can have various reflective shapes that direct the light downward. As demonstrated by the Reflector Study, the double parabola distributes the most light evenly.

Horizontal light reflectors can focus so much light on the garden that a hot spot can develop directly under the bulb. To dissipate this hot spot of light and lower the heat it creates, some manufacturers (Adjust-A-Wing and PL) install a light deflector below the bulb. The deflector helps spread the light and heat. The reflective hood can be placed even closer to the plants when there is no hot spot. We must again remind you of how fast light fades. If you are growing high light plants, this means that you get the absolute optimum efficiency from the bulb and reflector.

Reflectors that require lamps to hang vertically are less practical. When you hang a lamp vertically, much of its light is emitted out the sides and must strike the side of the hood before it is reflected downward to reach plants. When you have the choice between direct light and reflected light, direct light is more intense and therefore more economical. The light must also travel farther before being reflected in a vertical reflector compared to a horizontal reflector.

 **Rule of Thumb:** Horizontal reflectors are the most effective and the best all round value.

Parabolic dome reflectors are a fairly efficient type of vertical reflectors. The vertical parabolic dome reflector offers a relatively even light distribution, but throws less overall light than a horizontal reflector. Cone-shaped and other reflectors using a vertical bulb waste much light and are very inefficient. If you try to save money buying a cone shaped reflector (also called a Chinaman Hat) you will soon spend more money on electricity than you saved on the cone hood. When you reach the break even point, you will be stuck with a very inefficient reflective hood and actually lose money for every second the lamp is using electricity! (See Reflector Study)

Make sure that your hood is light-weight so you can hang it from the ceiling or garden bench. Aluminum reflectors are lightweight.

Some reflective hoods dissipate heat better than others. We recommend lightweight reflective hoods with open ends or plenty of vents to dissipate heat. Aluminum dissipates heat quicker than steel. If your reflective hood gets hot and dissipates heat slowly, train a fan on it to carry the heat

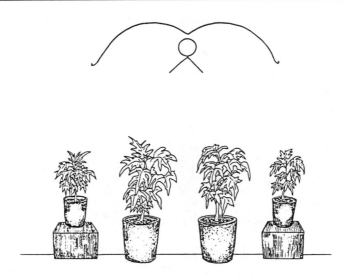

*Setting plants on a stand under the HID to retain an even garden profile.*

away.  Open ended hoods offer the added air flow directly through the hood and around the bulb.  This air flow cools the bulb and the fixture.

## Reflectant light

Many gardeners also paint the walls of their garden rooms white.  Ideally, place your plants twelve inches or less from the white reflective walls.  If possible, create moveable reflective walls which you can rotate around the plants.  This increases the amount of reflection.  Use a corner of a room as your garden area.  This way you can use the two walls of the corner as reflective walls.  You can construct the remaining two walls out of plywood, moisture resistant sheet rock, or white visqueen plastic.  Many gardeners have found that white visqueen plastic makes an ideal white-out substance.  It is inexpensive, lightweight and easy to remove and reuse.

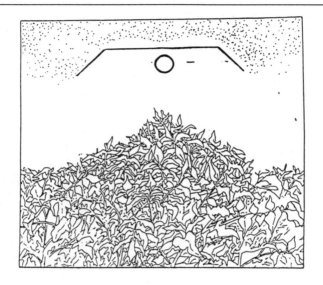

*This hood has a "hot spot" and plants grow into that area.*

*Different types of plants that need different amounts of light. Place plants at the proper distance from the light.*

It is a great material to use if you need to partition off your garden room. As your garden needs more space, it is easy to move the plastic. In addition, because the plastic is waterproof, you can use it on walls and floors. Do not use reflective white plastic on the floor, becaue the leave bottoms will burn from th reflected light. Because it is so mobile, it is easy to keep your walls close to your plants to provide optimum reflection.

When choosing between white visqueen plastic and flat white paint, there are several points to consider. White visqueen may be difficult to find, it is not as reflective as flat white paint and after several years can become brittle. But it can be readily fashioned into a moveable wall that can enclose a garden. This visqueen wall can be moved back as the garden grows. In Australia they use Hydrofilm (black/white on one side each). In heavier thicknesses, it works well to form a mobile wall.

If you opt to paint your garden room, you will have to choose between flat white, semi-gloss and titanium white paint. Each has advantages and disadvantages. Flat white paint is inexpensive and reflective. The average home garden room can be painted with flat white paint for under $25. Semi-gloss white paint is easier to wash but less reflective than flat white. Artist's white and titanium white paint are both more reflective and more expensive. To maximize your investment, use this more expensive paint on the hood itself, but a less expensive alternative on the walls of your garden area. Do not paint the floor white, the reflection is detrimental to tender leaf undersides. When painting your garden room, remember to apply a primer first and use a vent fan to avoid inhaling fumes. Although painting may be a messy alternative, it is worth it. It helps control fungus and moisture problems and significantly increases the usable growing space in your garden area.

If you opt to avoid the mess of paint and can not find white visqueen plastic, you can also use reflective mylar.

This material is highly reflective, reflecting between 90-95 % of the light.  To install reflective mylar, simply tape or tack it to the wall.  To prevent rips or tears, place a piece of tape over the spot where the staple, nail or tack will be inserted.  Be certain that it *lies flat* against the wall.  Any waves in the mylar will prevent optimum reflection and can cause bright spots.  Don't try to skimp and use aluminum foil instead of reflective mylar.  Aluminum foil actually wastes light because of its crinkles.  When light hits these crinkles, it is reflected in the wrong direction and never reaches the plants.  In addition, aluminum foil reflects more ultraviolet rays than other surfaces; it is harmfmul to-chloroplasts in leaves.  Mirrors are also an option, but actually reflect less light than mylar.  The light must first pass throught the mirror's glass, then be reflected and pass back through the glass.  Each time the light passes through the glass, light is lost.

## Light Distribution

        Providing an even distribution of light is an easy way to increase the productivity of your garden lights.  When your light distribution is uneven, most plants will grow towards the more intense light.  If your lights are stationary and have hot spots, plants will grow towards them.  This fosters uneven growth and plant shading.  Plants that grow towards and around a lamp will shade others and your garden will suffer.  Some gardeners install side lighting to help maintain good light distribution.  Installing side lights increases the amount of electricity you will use, but it also increases the amount of light available for your garden.  Other gardeners simply rotate their plants so that they receive full light.  They move the taller plants toward the outside of the garden and the smaller plants toward the center where light is more intense.  Another option is to set smaller plants on a stand so that the profile of the garden is evened

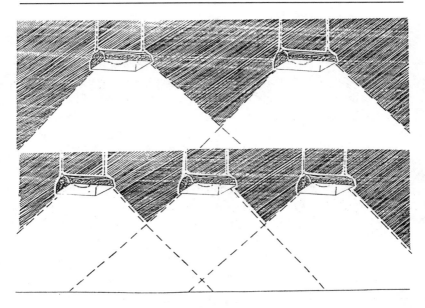

*Three 600-watt HP sodium lamps produce almost as much light as two 1000-watt HP sodium lamps and they can be placed closer to plants.*

out. You can also arrange plants in a concave shape (stadium method) under the lamp; the plants directly under the bulb are farthest away while the plants on the perimeter are closer. These options are less expensive, but also more labor intensive, especially if you have a large garden. You can place your planting containers on wheels to make your job less laborious.

 **Rule of Thumb:** Group your plants according to light needs, placing those that require a lower light intensity around the outside edge of your lighted garden area.

You can also take advantage of the different levels of light below the HID and place plants that require low light levels on the perimeter, medium light plants closer in and high light plants near the center of the garden. Use the same

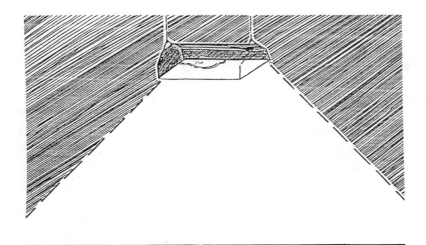

*One 600-watt HP sodium placed closer to plants can be more effective than a 1000-watt bulb placed farther away.*

principles indoor as apply outdoors.  If a plant needs filtered sun, place it where it receives filtered light from the HID.  If growing cuttings or seedlings that require lower light levels, place them on the parameter of the garden or shade them with a screen.

      Artificial light is most effective when it is emitted from more than one point.  Since light diminishes to the square of the distance, it fades very fast.  So the idea is to get the lamp as close as possible to the garden.  But when using a 1000-watt HID lamp that emminates lots of light, it also radiates lots of heat and the bulb must be farther away from the plants so the heat it produces does not burn them.  It is more effective to use smaller wattage bulbs, for example two 400 watt bulbs that can be placed closer to the plants rather than one 1000 watt bulb.  The disadvantage is that two 400 watt systems cost more than one 1000 watt system.  The benefits of using two 400 watt bulbs include:

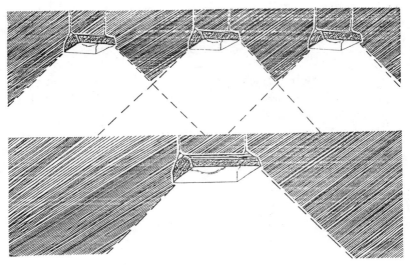

*Three 400-watt lamps are much better than one 1000-watt system. Three 400-watt lamps produce 1200 watts from three point sources to provide more even distribution of light. The 400-watt fixtures can also be placed closer to plants making most efficient use of bulb brilliance.*

1. More point sources of light
2. More even distribution of light
3. Light used more efficiently since it is closer to the plants.

   Some reflective hoods reflect light more evenly than others. A reflector that distributes light evenly, with no hot spots, can be placed closer to plants without burning them in a "hot spot". These hoods are most efficient because the lamp is closer and the light more intense. Remember light fades fast and the closer the light is to the plant, the better. The farther the lamp is from the garden, the less light plants receive. For example, a 1000-watt reflector with a "hot spot" must be placed 3 feet above the garden. While a 600-watt lamp with a reflector that distributes light evenly can be placed only 1.5 feet above the garden. The 600 watt system shines as much light on the garden as the 1000-watt system!!

# Light Reflector Study

The light reflector studies were a lot of fun to complete. They were also a lot of work! We proceeded with the studies in a simple straight forward way. We painted a room flat black, laid out a grid on 30 centimeter (11.7 inches) centers and humg a lamp and hood exactly one meter (from the bottom of the bulb) above the center point of the 9 square meter grid. We used the exact same bulb(s) of each diffrent wattage and type. Each bulb was warmed up for exactly 100 hours before used on the first test. We warmed the bulb up 20 minutes before taking each test. The tests were made with a Gossen Panlux light meter with new batteries. We took footcandle readings at each 30 centimeter (11.7 inches) point. These readings were then entered into a spreadsheet program. We used the computer and the information we gathered to make the light distribution graphs.

We suggest that you try your own light studies and check HID bulbs with a light meter each month. Make sure to take your readings at the same locations each month. As few as two or three points is enough if you are in a hurry. This is the simplest, surest way for you to get the most from your lighting.

We noticed one basic premise during the light studies. This simple fact is that the *wider* the distribution of *bright* light, the *closer* the lamp can be placed to plants, and the more efficient the light! See the drawing on page 17. It shows that light diminishes *very* quickly. For example light 3 feet from the bulb is only 1/9th as bright as light 1 foot away! This tells us that if you are growing bright light plants, use a reflector that spreads the bright light in a large patern over the garden.

If your garden requires various levels of light, use a reflector that has a hot spot of light in the middle and various levels of light around the parimeter. This way you can place plants in the level of light they need.

We called indoor garden stores around the world and asked them which bulbs they recommend. We found that horizontal bulbs are the choice hands down around the world. HP sodium bulbs are most often recommended in Australia, New Zealand and Europe. Indoor garden stores in the United States and Canada recommend both super metal halide and HP sodium lamps. We still do not know which lamp is best. We do know that some varieties of plants respond better to of blend of metal halide and HP sodium light. Other plant varieties respond well to HP sodium light and grow even better under the color corrected HP sodium bulbs.

We also found several very interesting tidbits of information, many of which are salted through this book. One gardener in Australia provided the following piece of advice.

If you use three 600-watt HP sodium lamps you get a total of 270,000 lumens at a cost of $0.18 per hour (cost per KWH = $0.10)

If you use 2-1000 watt HP sodium lamps, you get a total of 280,000 lumens at a cost of $0.20 per hour.

The cost of running three 600 watts is less than running two HP sodiums. The 600 watt bulbs generate more lumens for the same amount of money, and can be placed closer toplants, plus there is the added benefit of having three point sources of light. The more point sources, the more even the distribution of light. The 600 watt systems offer a much better choice over the 2 HP sodium systems. Of course three 600 watt systems cost more than two 1000 watt HP sodium systems.

The last thing we noticed so far was the amazing showing of the parabolic dome reflector using a vertical bulb. It spreads the light quite well!

We would like to thank all the manufacturers and suppliers that sent us their reflective hoods to participate in this study. The bulbs were supplied by Hydrofarm and Sunlite Supply. Transformers and were supplied by Hydrofarm. We used the same transformers throughout the study.

Suppliers did not send in all the reflective hoods they cary. Brite Lite, for example, sent only the economy reflectors they handle.

This index is only a basic measure of the spread of light for a specific light reflector. Overall light is only taken into account in relation to the amount of light directly under the bulb. To get a complete understanding of the amount and distribution of light, you must study the graph, overall amount of light, amount of light under the bulb and the "V" Index for each reflective hood.

To figure the "V" Index, divide the total amount of foot-candles in a 9 square meter area by the total amount of foot-candles in the 1.2 meter area directly below the bulb.

**Manufacturer:** Hydrofarm    **Relfector** = - Sunburst
**Orientation** = Horizontal    **Bulb:** 250-watt HPS
**Characteristics** = Dual parabola **fc in 9 sq m** = 171890
**Finish** = pebble specular    **fc under bulb** = 116160
**Shape** = rectangle, attached    (in1.2 sq m)
   balast    **"V" Index** = 1.47

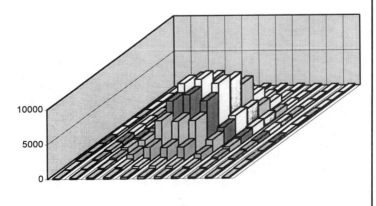

**Manufacturer:** Ablite/Hydrofarm  **Relfector** = Adjust-A-Wing
**Orientation** = Horizontal  **Bulb:** 400-watt HPS
**Characteristics** = Dual parabola  **fc in 9 sq m** = 202208
**Finish** = white  **fc under bulb** = 95080
**Shape** = Wing  (in1.2 sq m)
**"V" Index** = 2.12

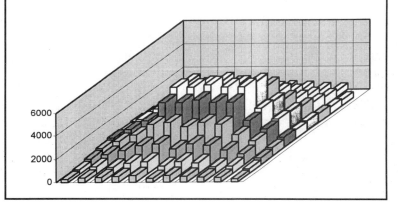

**Manufacturer:** Accent Hydro.  **Relfector** = White Wing
**Orientation** = Horizontal  **Bulb:** 400-watt HPS
**Characteristics** = Angular dual  **fc in 9 sq m** = 185492
parabola  **fc under bulb** = 98480
**Finish** = Hammer specular  (in1.2 sq m)
**Shape** = Wing  **"V" Index** = 1.88

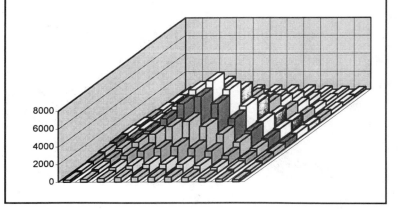

**Manufacturer:** Accent Hydro.
**Orientation** = Horizontal
**Characteristics** = Angular dual parabola
**Finish** = Hammer specular
**Shape** = Wing

**Relfector** = Silver Wing
**Bulb:** 400-watt HPS
**fc in 9 sq m** = 195054
**fc under bulb** = 109960
   (in 1.2 sq m)
**"V" Index** = 1.77

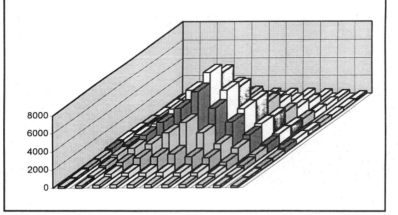

**Manufacturer:** Allie's Wholesale
**Orientation** = Horizontal
**Characteristics** = Angular sides, flat top,
**Finish** = white
**Shape** = Rectangle

**Relfector** = Small Horiz.
**Bulb:** 400-watt HPS
**fc in 9 sq m** = 233326
**fc under bulb** = 128420
   (in 1.2 sq m)
**"V" Index** = 1.81

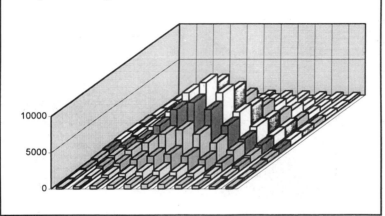

**Manufacturer:** Alternative Garden **Relfector** = "W"  (Wide)
**Orientation** = Horizontal          **Bulb:** 400-watt HPS
**Characteristics** = Double          **fc in 9 sq m** = 145998
parabola                              **fc under bulb** = 58940
**Finish** = Anodized aluminum          (in1.2 sq m)
**Shape** = Rectangle                 **"V" Index** = 2.47

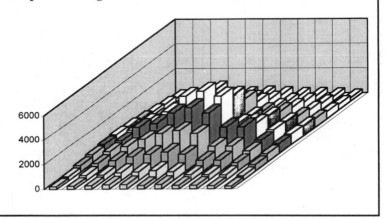

**Manufacturer:** Alternative Garden **Relfector** = "M" (Medium)
**Orientation** = Horizontal          **Bulb:** 400-watt HPS
**Characteristics** = Dual parabola   **fc in 9 sq m** = 211260
**Finish** = Anodized aluminum        **fc under bulb** = 90620
**Shape** = Octagon                     (in1.2 sq m)
                                      **"V" Index** = 2.33

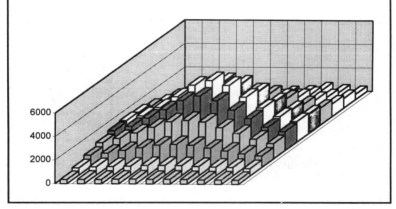

**Manufacturer:** Brite Lite
**Orientation** = Horizontal
**Characteristics** = Angular dual parabola
**Finish** = Mirror
**Shape** = Wing

**Reflector** = Horiz. Mirror
**Bulb:** 400-watt HPS
**fc in 9 sq m** = 216352
**fc under bulb** = 122980
    (in 1.2 sq m)
**"V" Index** = 1.75

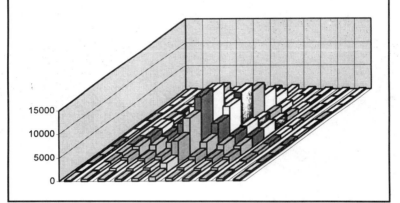

**Manufacturer:** Brite Lite
**Orientation** = Horizontal
**Characteristics** = Angular dual parabola, open end
**Finish** = White
**Shape** = Wing

**Relfector** = Horiz. Optimum
**Bulb:** 400-watt HPS
**fc in 9 sq m** = 173398
**fc under bulb** = 91510
    (in 1.2 sq m)
**"V" Index** = 1.89

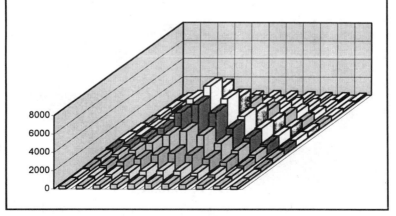

**Manufacturer:** Gro-Lite Australia    **Relfector** = Mirror Finish
**Orientation** = Horizontal            **Bulb:** 400-watt HPS
**Characteristics** = Angle/dual         **fc in 9 sq m** = 216572
parabola                                 **fc under bulb** = 132120
**Finish** = Mirror                         (in1.2 sq m)
**Shape** =  Wing                        **"V" Index** = 1.64

**Manufacturer:** Gro-Lite Australia    **Relfector** = Hammer Alum.
**Orientation** = Horizontal            **Bulb:** 400-watt HPS
**Characteristics** = Angle/dual         **fc in 9 sq m** = 216092
parabola                                 **fc under bulb** = 137880
**Finish** = Hammer specular                (in1.2 sq m)
**Shape** =  Wing                        **"V" Index** = 1.56

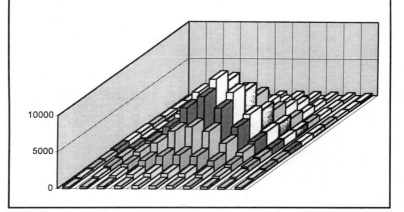

**Manufacturer:** Gro-Lite Australia
**Orientation** = Horizontal
**Characteristics** = Flat top, angular sides
**Finish** = Hammer Specular
**Shape** = Rectangle

**Relfector** = Megabright
**Bulb:** 400-watt HPS
**fc in 9 sq m** = 215820
**fc under bulb** = 131420
  (in 1.2 sq m)
**"V" Index** = 1.64

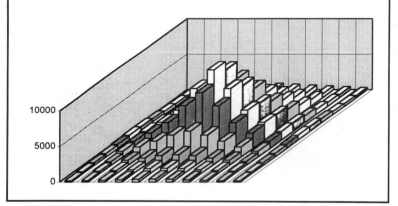

**Manufacturer:** Hydrofarm
**Orientation** = Horizontal
**Characteristics** = Parabolic, flat top
**Finish** = Pebble specular
**Shape** = Rectangle

**Relfector** = Grow Wing
**Bulb:** 400-watt HPS
**fc in 9 sq m** = 243580
**fc under bulb** = 160060
  (in 1.2 sq m)
**"V" Index** = 1.52

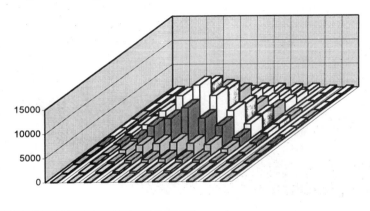

**Manufacturer:** Hydrofarm
**Orientation** = Horizontal
**Characteristics** = Dual parabola
**Finish** = Pebble specular
**Shape** = Rectangle, sloped sides

**Relfector** = Horiz. Parabola
**Bulb:** 400-watt HPS
**fc in 9 sq m** = 244872
**fc under bulb** = 152050
  (in 1.2 sq m)
**"V" Index** = 1.61

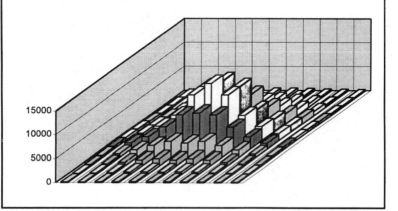

**Manufacturer:** Hydrofarm
**Orientation** = Horizontal
**Characteristics** = Dual
  parabola
**Finish** = Pebble specular
**Shape** = Rectangle, sloped
sides, attached ballast

**Relfector** = Sunburst
**Bulb:** 430-watt HPS
**fc in 9 sq m** = 292848
**fc under bulb** = 207220
  (in 1.2 sq m)
**"V" Index** = 1.41

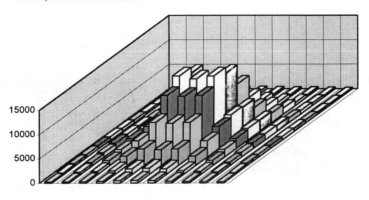

**Manufacturer:** Allies Wholesale
**Orientation** = Horizontal
**Characteristics** = Flat top, angular sides
**Finish** = White
**Shape** = Rectangle

**Relfector** = LRMV - Small
**Bulb:** 400-watt MS
**fc in 9 sq m** = 137600
**fc under bulb** = 73900
  (in1.2 sq m)
**"V" Index** = 1.86

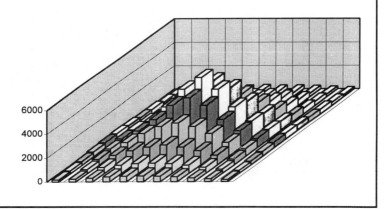

**Manufacturer:** AquaCulture
**Orientation** = Horizontal
**Characteristics** = Dual parabola
**Finish** = White
**Shape** = parabola, rectangle

**Relfector** = BrightStar
**Bulb:** 400-watt MS
**fc in 9 sq m** = 137326
**fc under bulb** = 79420
  (in1.2 sq m)
**"V" Index** = 1.72

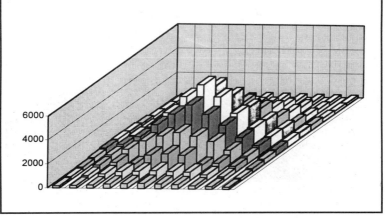

**Manufacturer:** Brite Lite
**Orientation** = Vertical
**Characteristics** = Cone
**Finish** = Mirror
**Shape** = Cone

**Relfector** = China Hat
**Bulb:** 400-watt MS
**fc in 9 sq m** = 165532
**fc under bulb** = 87460
  (in 1.2 sq m)
**"V" Index** = 1.89

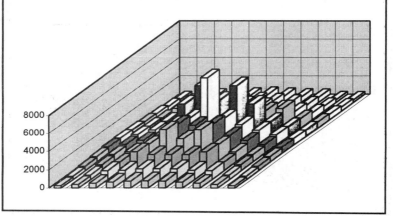

**Manufacturer:** Hydrofarm
**Orientation** = Horizontal
**Characteristics** = Double parabola
**Finish** = Pebble specular
**Shape** = Rectangle

**Relfector** = Grow Wing
**Bulb:** 400-watt MS
**fc in 9 sq m** = 152580
**fc under bulb** = 101080
  (in 1.2 sq m)
**"V" Index** = 1.51

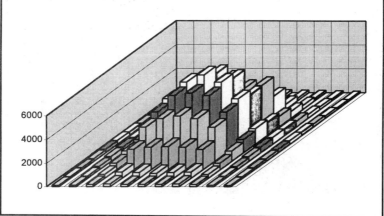

**Manufacturer:** Sunlite Supply
**Orientation** = Horizontal
**Characteristics** = Flat top, angular sides
**Finish** = White
**Shape** = Rectangle

**Relfector** = Small Horiz.
**Bulb:** 400-watt MS
**fc in 9 sq m** = 55662
**fc under bulb** = 36492
   (in 1.2 sq m)
**"V" Index** = 1.52

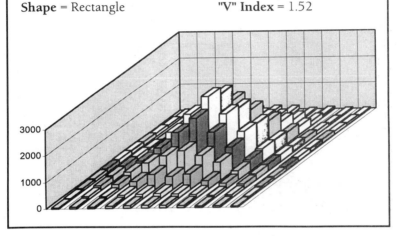

**Manufacturer:** Sunlite Supply
**Orientation** = Vertical
**Characteristics** = Parabolic dome
**Finish** = White
**Shape** = Dome

**Relfector** = Parabolic Dome
**Bulb:** 400-watt MS
**fc in 9 sq m** = 157680
**fc under bulb** = 71900
   (in 1.2 sq m)
**"V" Index** = 2.19

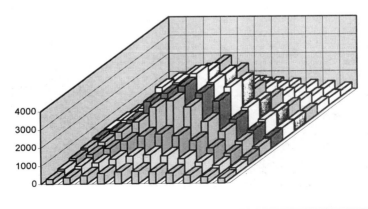

**Manufacturer:** Ablite/Hydrofarm   **Relfector** = Adjust-A-Wing
**Orientation** = Horizontal          **Bulb:** 600-watt HPS
**Characteristics** = Dual parabola   **fc in 9 sq m** = 351200
**Finish** = White                    **fc under bulb** = 180340
**Shape** = Wing                          (in1.2 sq m)
                                      **"V" Index** = 1.94

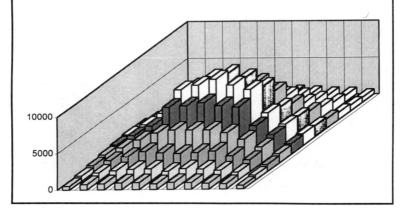

**Manufacturer:** Accent Hydro.      **Relfector** = White Wing
**Orientation** = Horizontal          **Bulb:** 600-watt HPS
**Characteristics** = Angular wing    **fc in 9 sq m** = 338260
**Finish** = White                    **fc under bulb** = 194800
**Shape** = Wing                          (in1.2 sq m)
                                      **"V" Index** = 1.73

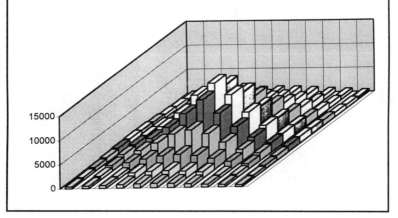

**Manufacturer:** Alternative Garden **Relfector** = "M" (Medium)
**Orientation** = Horizontal          **Bulb:** 600-watt HPS
**Characteristics** = dual parabola    **fc in 9 sq m** = 419360
**Finish** = Anodized aluminum         **fc under bulb** = 196580
**Shape** = Octagon                      (in1.2 sq m)
                                       **"V" Index** = 2.13

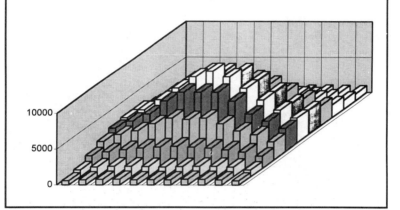

**Manufacturer:** Alternative Garden **Relfector** = "W" (Wide)
**Orientation** = Horizontal          **Bulb:** 600-watt HPS
**Characteristics** = Dual parabola    **fc in 9 sq m** = 286640
**Finish** = Anodized aluminum         **fc under bulb** = 144560
**Shape** = Rectangle                    (in1.2 sq m)
                                       **"V" Index** = 1.98

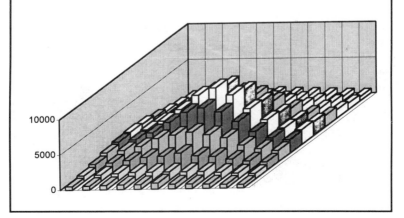

**Manufacturer:** Growth Tech.
**Orientation** = Horizontal
**Characteristics** = Dual parabola
**Finish** = Hammered specular
**Shape** = Rectangle

**Relfector** = Supernova
**Bulb:** 600-watt HPS
**fc in 9 sq m** = 406840
**fc under bulb** = 229000
  (in1.2 sq m)
**"V" Index** = 1.77

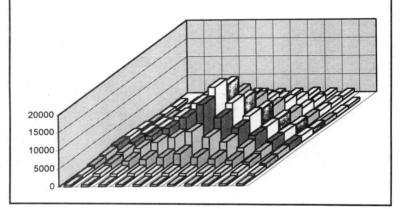

**Manufacturer:** Growth Tech.
**Orientation** = Horizontal
**Characteristics** = Dual parabola
**Finish** = White
**Shape** = Rectangle

**Relfector** = Supernova
**Bulb:** 600-watt HPS
**fc in 9 sq m** = 384792
**fc under bulb** = 250840
  (in1.2 sq m)
**"V" Index** = 1.53

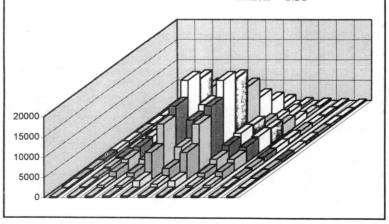

**Manufacturer:** Hydrofarm
**Orientation** = Horizontal
**Characteristics** = Dual parabola
**Finish** = Hammer specular
**Shape** = Rectangle

**Relfector** = Grow Wing
**Bulb:** 600-watt HPS
**fc in 9 sq m** = 436196
**fc under bulb** = 271240
  (in1.2 sq m)
**"V" Index** = 1.60

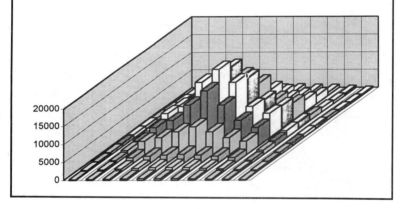

**Manufacturer:** Ablite/Hydrofarm
**Orientation** = Horizontal
**Characteristics** = Dual parabola
**Finish** = White
**Shape** = Wing

**Relfector** = Adjust-A-Wing
**Bulb:** 1000-watt HPS
**fc in 9 sq m** = 612880
**fc under bulb** = 315600
    (in1.2 sq m)
**"V" Index** = 1.94

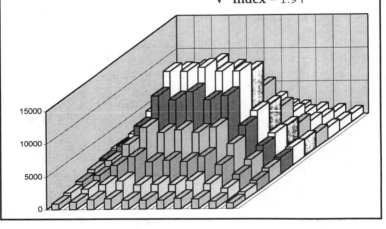

**Manufacturer:** Accent Hydro.
**Orientation** = Horizontal
**Characteristics** = Flat top, angular sides, open end
**Finish** = White
**Shape** = Rectangle

**Relfector** = Horizontal
**Bulb:** 1000-watt HPS
**fc in 9 sq m** = 595640
**fc under bulb** = 338800
    (in1.2 sq m)
**"V" Index** = 1.75

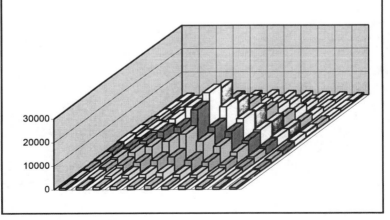

**Manufacturer:** Accent Hydro.
**Orientation** = Horizontal
**Characteristics** = Flat top, angular sides, closed end
**Finish** = White
**Shape** = Rectangle

**Relfector** = Horizontal
**Bulb:** 1000-watt HPS
**fc in 9 sq m** = 698260
**fc under bulb** = 417200
  (in1.2 sq m)
**"V" Index** = 1.67

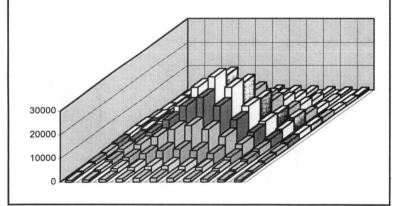

**Manufacturer:** Allie's Wholesale
**Orientation** = Horizontal
**Characteristics** = Flat top, angular sides
**Finish** = White
**Shape** = Rectangle

**Relfector** = LR - Large
**Bulb:** 1000-watt HPS
**fc in 9 sq m** = 511860
**fc under bulb** = 290400
  (in1.2 sq m)
**"V" Index** = 1.76

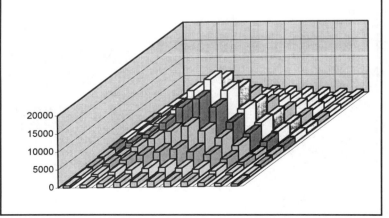

**Manufacturer:** AquaCulture      **Relfector** = BrightStar
**Orientation** = Horizontal       **Bulb:** 1000-watt HPS
**Characteristics** = Dual parabola  **fc in 9 sq m** = 650080
**Finish** = White                 **fc under bulb** = 366400
**Shape** = Rectangle                 (in1.2 sq m)
                                   **"V" Index** = 1.77

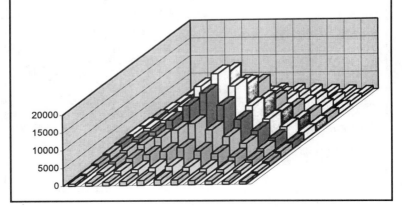

**Manufacturer:** Brite Lite       **Relfector** = Horiz. Optimum
**Orientation** = Horizontal       **Bulb:** 1000-watt HPS
**Characteristics** = Angular dual  **fc in 9 sq m** = 530920
parabola, open end                 **fc under bulb** = 280400
**Finish** = White                    (in1.2 sq m)
**Shape** = Wing                   **"V" Index** = 1.89

**Manufacturer:** Brite Lite
**Orientation** = Horizontal
**Characteristics** = Angular dual
parabola, open end
**Finish** = Mirror
**Shape** = Wing

**Relfector** = Horiz. Mirror
**Bulb:** 1000-watt HPS
**fc in 9 sq m** = 661240
**fc under bulb** = 409600
(in 1.2 sq m)
**"V" Index** = 1.61

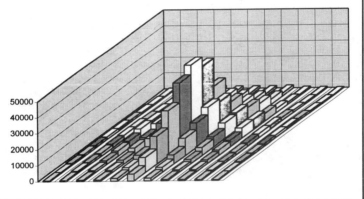

**Manufacturer:** Diamond Lights
**Orientation** = Horizontal
**Characteristics** = Angular dual
parabola
**Finish** = Dull mirror
**Shape** = Rectangle

**Relfector** = Horizontal II
**Bulb:** 1000-watt HPS
**fc in 9 sq m** = 633000
**fc under bulb** = 424300
(in 1.2 sq m)
**"V" Index** = 1.49

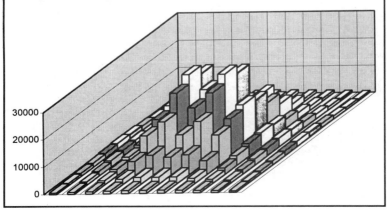

**Manufacturer:** East Coast Hydro.   **Relfector** = Ross Special
**Orientation** = Horizontal          **Bulb:** 1000-watt HPS
**Characteristics** = Angular dual    **fc in 9 sq m** = 669530
parabola, open end                    **fc under bulb** = 388900
**Finish** = Mirror                       (in1.2 sq m)
**Shape** = Wing                      **"V" Index** = 1.72

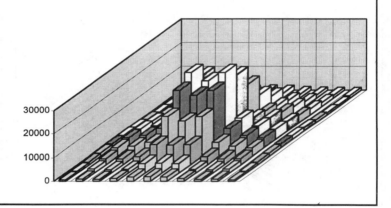

**Manufacturer:** Green Air Prod.     **Relfector** = Horizontal
**Orientation** = Horizontal          **Bulb:** 1000-watt HPS
**Characteristics** = Flat top, angu- **fc in 9 sq m** = 645580
lar sides, glass shield               **fc under bulb** = 391200
**Finish** = White                        (in1.2 sq m)
**Shape** = Rectangle                 **"V" Index** = 1.65

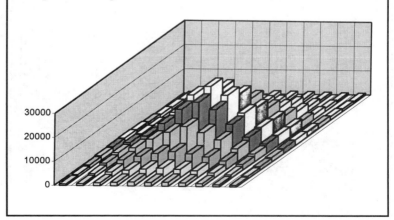

**Manufacturer:** Green Air Prod.
**Orientation** = Horizontal
**Characteristics** = Flat top, angular sides, no glass shield
**Finish** = White
**Shape** = Rectangle

**Relfector** = Horizontal
**Bulb:** 1000-watt HPS
**fc in 9 sq m** = 669740
**fc under bulb** = 397600
(in 1.2 sq m)
**"V" Index** = 1.68

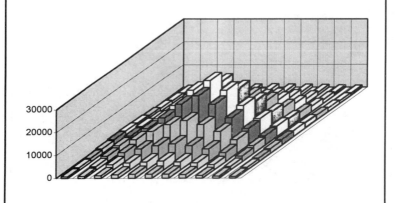

**Manufacturer:** Greentrees
**Orientation** = Horizontal
**Characteristics** = Angular dual parabola
**Finish** = Mirror
**Shape** = Rectangle

**Relfector** = Everbright
**Bulb:** 1000-watt HPS
**fc in 9 sq m** = 686080
**fc under bulb** = 424000
(in 1.2 sq m)
**"V" Index** = 1.61

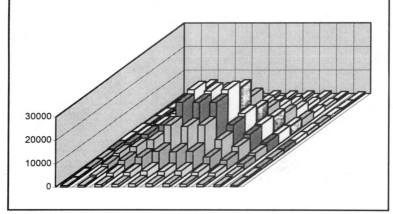

**Manufacturer:** Gro-Lite Australia  **Relfector** = Mirror Finish
**Orientation** = Horizontal  **Bulb:** 1000-watt HPS
**Characteristics** = Angular dual  **fc in 9 sq m** = 783360
parabola, round sides, open end  **fc under bulb** = 492160
**Finish** = Mirror  (in 1.2 sq m)
**Shape** = Wing  **"V" Index** = 1.59

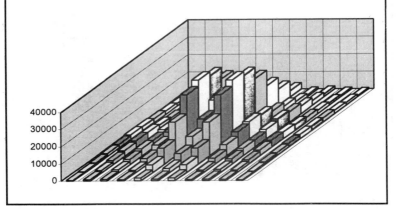

**Manufacturer:** Hydrofarm  **Relfector** = Grow Wing
**Orientation** = Horizontal  **Bulb:** 1000-watt HPS
**Characteristics** = Dual parabola  **fc in 9 sq m** = 767400
**Finish** = Pebble specular  **fc under bulb** = 454200
**Shape** = Rectangle  (in 1.2 sq m)
**"V" Index** = 1.69

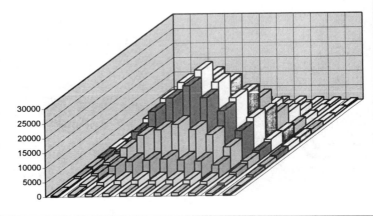

**Manufacturer:** Hydrofarm
**Orientation** = Horizontal
**Characteristics** = Flat top, parabola
**Finish** = Pebble specular
**Shape** = Octagon

**Relfector** = Horiz. Parabola
**Bulb:** 1000-watt HPS
**fc in 9 sq m** = 452496
**fc under bulb** = 198820
  (in 1.2 sq m)
**"V" Index** = 1.51

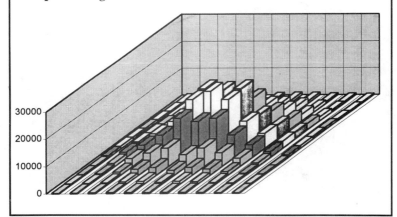

**Manufacturer:** Superior Grower's
**Orientation** = Horizontal
**Characteristics** = Dual parabola
**Finish** = Hammer specular
**Shape** = Rectangle

**Relfector** = Horizontal
**Bulb:** 1000-watt HPS
**fc in 9 sq m** = 765920
**fc under bulb** = 497800
  (in 1.2 sq m)
**"V" Index** = 1.53

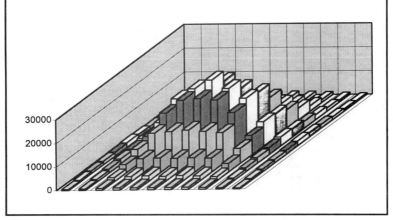

**Manufacturer:** Allie's Wholesale
**Orientation** = Horizontal
**Characteristics** = Flat top angular sides
**Finish** = White
**Shape** = Rectangle

**Relfector** = LR - Large
**Bulb:** 1000-watt MS
**fc in 9 sq m** = 559540
**fc under bulb** = 313900
   (in 1.2 sq m)
**"V" Index** = 1.78

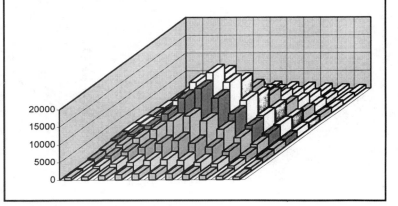

**Manufacturer:** Brite Lite
**Orientation** = Vertical
**Characteristics** = Cone
**Finish** = Mirror
**Shape** = Cone

**Relfector** = China Hat
**Bulb:** 1000-watt MS
**fc in 9 sq m** = 460970
**fc under bulb** = 234800
   (in 1.2 sq m)
**"V" Index** = 1.96

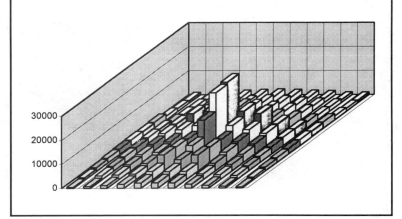

**Manufacturer:** Diamond Lights
**Orientation** = Horizontal
**Characteristics** = Dual parabola
**Finish** = Hammer specular
**Shape** = Rectangle

**Relfector** = Horizontal II
**Bulb:** 1000-watt MS
**fc in 9 sq m** = 464880
**fc under bulb** = 322000
    (in1.2 sq m)
**"V" Index** = 1.44

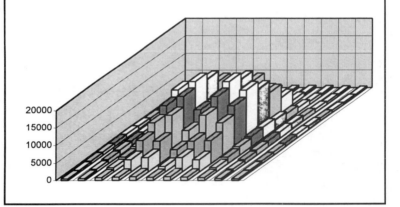

**Manufacturer:** Greentrees
**Orientation** = Horizontal
**Characteristics** = Angular dual-parabola
**Finish** = Mirror
**Shape** = Rectangle

**Relfector** = Everbright
**Bulb:** 1000-watt MS
**fc in 9 sq m** = 475160
**fc under bulb** = 285000
    (in1.2 sq m)
**"V" Index** = 1.66

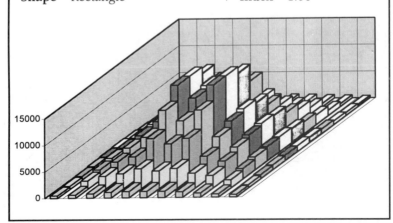

**Manufacturer:** Hydrofarm          **Relfector** = Grow Wing
**Orientation** = Horizontal          **Bulb:** 1000-watt MS
**Characteristics** = Dual parabola   **fc in 9 sq m** = 571380
**Finish** = Pebble specular          **fc under bulb** = 370400
**Shape** = Rectangle                     (in1.2 sq m)
                                      **"V" Index** = 1.54

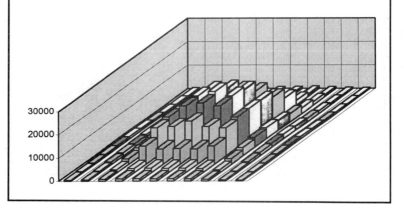

**Manufacturer:** Sunlight Supply    **Relfector** = Parabolic Dome
**Orientation** = Vertical           **Bulb:** 1000-watt MS
**Characteristics** = Parabolic dome **fc in 9 sq m** = 434020
**Finish** = White                   **fc under bulb** = 186200
**Shape** = Octagon                      (in1.2 sq m)
                                     **"V" Index** = 2.33

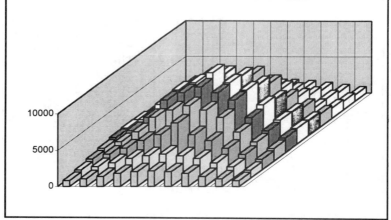

**Manufacturer:** Sunlight Supply
**Orientation** = Vertical
**Characteristics** = Flat round
**Finish** = White
**Shape** = Flat cone

**Relfector** = Flat Cone
**Bulb:** 1000-watt MS
**fc in 9 sq m** = 299330
**fc under bulb** = **134940**
  (in1.2 sq m)
**"V" Index** = 2.21

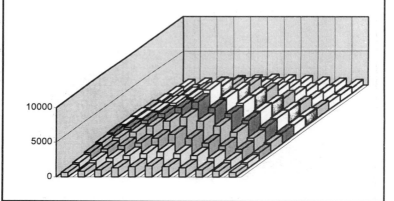

**Manufacturer:** Sunlight Supply
**Orientation** = Horizontal
**Characteristics** = Flat top, angular sides
**Finish** = White
**Shape** = Rectangle

**Relfector** = Horizontal
**Bulb:** 1000-watt MS
**fc in 9 sq m** = 547240
**fc under bulb** = 301820
  (in1.2 sq m)
**"V" Index** = 1.81

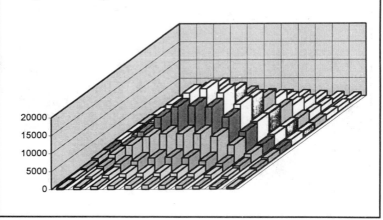

**Manufacturer:** Sunlight Supply     **Relfector** = Cone
**Orientation** = Vertical            **Bulb:** 1000-watt MS
**Characteristics** = Cone            **fc in 9 sq m** = 369640
**Finish** = White                    **fc under bulb** = 15220
**Shape** = Cone                        (in1.2 sq m)
                                      **"V" Index** = 2.42

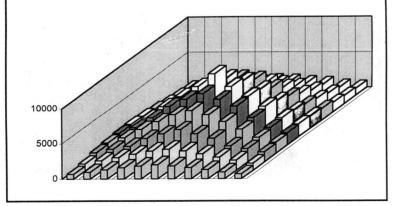

**Manufacturer:** Superior Grower's **Relfector** = Horizontal
**Orientation** = Horizontal          **Bulb:** 1000-watt MS
**Characteristics** = Dual parabola   **fc in 9 sq m** = 551200
**Finish** = Hammer specular          **fc under bulb** = 343200
**Shape** = Rectangle                   (in1.2 sq m)
                                      **"V" Index** = 1.60

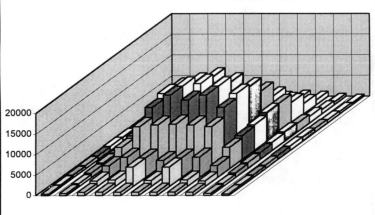

## Light Movers

A less labor intensive option than moving plants is to purchase a light mover. Light movers move garden lights across or around the ceiling of the garden room so the light covers more surface area. In effect, the objective of a light mover is to replicate the sun's movement. With the light moving above the garden, each plant will receive more direct, intense light. For best results, do not use a light mover on fast growing annuals or vegetables until they are 12 inches tall and have several sets of leaves. If you employ a light mover for young cuttings or seedlings, they might stretch towards the light and become leggy.

Light movers are a good value to use with hoods that have "hot spots". They distribute intense light more evenly to more of the garden. With a light mover, you can get bright lights closer to plants with less chance of burning leaves.

According to several manufacturers, you can use fewer lamps than you would with a stationary system and still expect the same yield. In fact, light movers increase intense light coverage by 25-35 percent. Two lamps mounted on a light mover will perform the job of three stationary lights. If you can afford a commercially-made motorized unit, they are the best for maintaining an even garden profile.

Light movers are available commercially in two styles: linear and circular. Homemade models can be manually operated while commercial light movers are motorized. As a general rule, the more often a light crosses over the garden, the more even the light distribution will be. Although it is not important if the light mover replicates the sun's east to west direction, it should replicate the sun's consistency. Motorized units regulate themselves to maintain this consistency. For manual units, establish a schedule and abide by it. If the lamp remains in the same position for several days before it is moved, plants will not receive even light distribution.

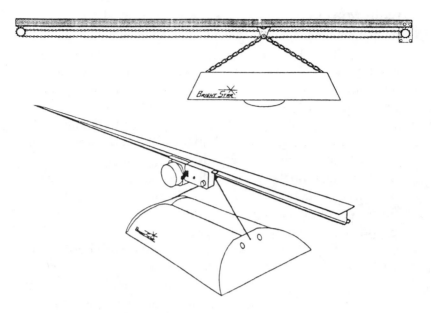

*AquaCulture developed the first light mover known as the Solar Shuttle (above). Their newest light mover is called the StarTrak (below).*

Regardless of whether your light mover is manually or mechanically operated, it moves in either a straight line or a circle. Liner systems increase light intensity in a linear oval. The length of track, number, wattage and type of lamps used determines the square footage covered by the system. According to one manufacturer, A six-foot linear light mover (using a 1000 watt lamp) increases optimum coverage of light from 36 to 72 square feet. Linear systems run on a track that is secured to the ceiling. The track guides the lamp as it moves across the ceiling. Depending on your lighting needs, you can purchase tracks that move up to six lamps at once. Lamps are attached to the track with an extendible chain or cord so lights can be positioned at varying heights depending on the plants' growth stage.

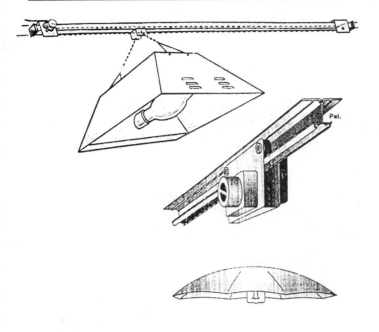

*Hydrofarm's Light Track (above) and Gualala Robotics' Light Rail III (below) are two popular light movers.*

Light movers that move in a 360 degree circle cover slightly more area than their linear counterparts. Both linear and circular units suspend lamps from adjustable chains.

For a manually operated linear track system, some gardeners construct a clothesline unit. Simply attach eye-bolts to the ceiling at opposite ends of your garden room. Attach pulleys to the eyebolts and string a heavy-duty nylon cord in a loop between the pulleys. Attach your lamp to the bottom of the loop and you will be able to move the lamp as often as desired— the more the better.

Now that you understand the basics of light and how to maximize your lighting investment, you are ready to choose a lighting system that best suits your needs. Artificial light applied in a prudent manner will stimulate growth,

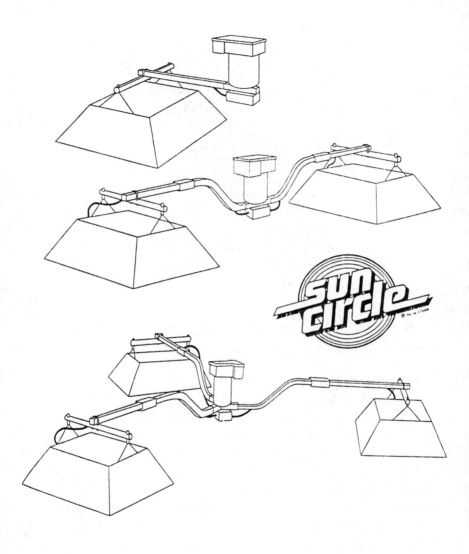

*The Sun Circle light movers, manufactured by American Hydroponics, are the standard for circular light movers.*

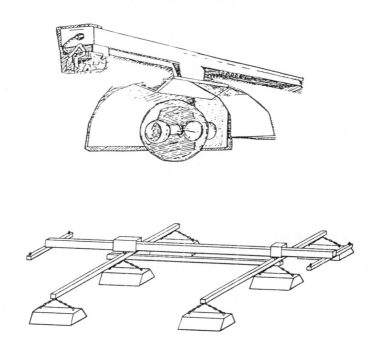

*The Pro-Track II, manufactured by Rambridge, Canada (above) is a popular light mover. The Jupiter II models by Ireland's Hydroponics, Australia can move up to six 6 lights.*

shorten production cycles, harbor healthier plants and promote earlier flowering. Remember, pay careful attention to your gardening needs when you are selecting a lighting system. You may consider using different types of lights for different growth stages. For instance, a lamp that is ideal for seedlings and cuttings such as a 175-watt metal halide may not be ideal for mature plants. If you garden in a sunny spot, you will be able to make use of natural light during the day and supplement with artificial light at night.

# Chapter Five:
# Choosing the Right Lighting System

Before purchasing a lighting system, consider all of your lighting needs and choose a system which best meets the majority of them. Consider the type of light emitted, the uniformity of light distribution, efficiency, cost and ease of maintenance. To determine a lamp's efficiency, look up its LPW conversion on the Light Bulb Chart. When considering cost, look not only at the initial installation cost, but also at longevity and replacement costs for bulbs. For example, a Philips phosphor coated (ED28 bulb) 400 watt metal halide costs less to buy than a Philips clear (ED37 bulb) 400-watt super metal halide. But the phosphor bulb is rated for an average life of 12,000 hours and produces 28,800 mean lumens. The super bulb is rated for an average life of 20,000 hours and produces 32,000 mean lumens. Both bulbs use the exact same amount of electricity! Which bulb would you rather own? To get a better idea of which bulb is best for your needs, study the Light Bulb Chart. Not all bulbs are created equal!

There are many lights available to indoor gardeners. Some lights should not be used at all. Other bulbs have distinct advantages and there is a small group of lamps that shine brighter than all others. After reading the next few pages, you should be able to access your needs and successfully choose a lighting system, or a combination of lighting systems, for your garden. The objective is to choose the most economical system which will reap the greatest benefit for your plants.

 **Rule of Thumb:** Not all light bulbs are created equal! Study the Light Bulb Charts before buying your next bulb.

You can purchase HID systems with wattages of 150, 175, 250, 400, 430, 600 and 1000 watts. HIDs are available in many more wattages. We listed only the most effective for plant growth. Remember, the higher the watts, the brighter the light and the more growing space provided. In general, the higher watts also mean higher electric bills. Although the 1000-watt system costs close to 30 percent more than the 400-watt system, overall it has a higher lumen-per-watt conversion and produces more than twice as much light. For a small greenhouse room, or a grow space that is less than 16 square feet, the 400-watt system is preferable. A 1000 watt bulb will shed light on 36 to 100 square feet while a 400 watt lamp will cover 16 to 25 feet. (see Light Reflector Studies in Chapter Four) 175 and 250 watt bulbs cover four to nine square feet with intense light. If you are growing low-light plants, you can either raise the lamp, or use a smaller bulb.

## Specific Applications

As you now know, HID lamps have many practical horticultural applications. You can install a 150-watt metal halide bulb in your living space to display  plants and/or to supplement the light it receives. Metal halides are preferred for living spaces because they emit a balanced "white" light which is flattering to plants and pleasing to the human eye. Sodium bulbs, on the other hand, emit a yellow light which many people prefer to relegate only to their garden rooms.

Even when you have narrowed your selection down to one type of HID, you still must consider how many watts you need. For instance, if you decide that high pressure sodium bulbs best suit your needs, you now need to determine how many watts the system you purchase should have. If you want to hang the light on a sun porch where the garden receives natural light, you might select a 400-watt HP sodium system. Because plants on a sun porch or greenhouse receive well-balanced light from the sun, you do not need to worry about providing additional blue light to supplement HPS's yellow and red light.

However, if you grow your plants in a dark basement room which receives no natural sunlight, you will need both a more intense light and a means of providing a fuller spectrum. You might choose a color corrected HPS bulb such as the SON AGRO or you might choose to install both a HPS and a metal halide system to ensure well-balanced spectral distribution.

A 1000-watt system might work well for plants in their vegetative growth stage, but seedlings and cuttings would fry under such intensity. For propagation, you should look to a 175-watt metal halide system. In this instance, you might start with a metal halide system to encourage photosynthesis and prevent legginess. As the plant matures, you might switch to a high pressure sodium conversion bulb to provide extra yellow and red light and promote flowering. Your choices are endless.

If you are confused about what kind of light to offer your plants, consult the Light Bulb charts. They will help you to narrow down your choices. Low-light plants will not thrive directly under 1000-watt bulbs, while high-light plants will grow very well. Once you have decided what you want to grow and what the most favorable growing conditions are for that species, cross-reference that information with the charts and information this book provides about different

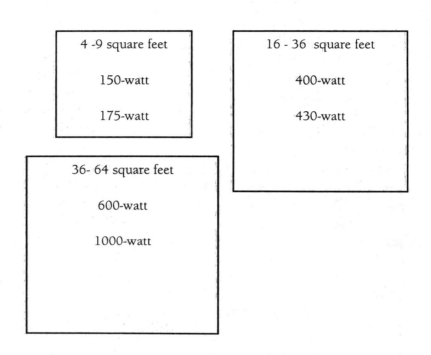

*These boxes show the approximate space different lamps illuminate.*

HID lights.  By doing this, you will be able to accurately meet your plants needs and therefore reap the greatest rewards for your garden investment.

## Using Artificial Light in a Greenhouse

If you have a greenhouse or a sunroom full of plants, you can hang a HP sodium lamp from the ceiling to grow a super garden through the dreary months of winter.  During cloudy months of fall winter and spring, the sun is not as bright, there are more clouds and the days are shorter.  The HP sodium will change all of these limiting growth factors.

*HP sodium lamp set up in a greenhouse*

Photo switches are available from several manufacturers including Green Air Products that will turn the HP sodium lamp on and off when light falls below a specified level. This means that on a cloudy day in the winter when there is barely enough light for a fern to grow, the photo switch will turn on the HID. This photo switch is similar to the type that turns street lights and security lights on and off at dusk.

For example, several studies have shown better yields when artificial light is applied at low levels for sustained periods of time, as opposed to at high levels for short periods. The effectiveness of artificial light is determined not only by the intensity and duration of time it is applied, but also by the degree to which the artificial light supplements sunlight. By paying attention to how much artificial light augments natural sunlight, you can determine just how much it helps your garden grow.

We have also heard of empirical studies using only artificial light that support the above studies. The following example assumes that plants wake up slowly. In these tests, several gardeners using light movers with three lights would turn on one of the lights, a super metal halide, for the first hour in the morning. They would then turn on the other two lights, HP sodiums, during the rest of the day. The gardeners did not notice any change in growth of their garden. In theory this principle makes sense. Nonetheless, this information comes from only a few experiments that some gardeners completed. We would like to see more information about similar studies.

## Setting Up a Lighting System

There are many ways to set up your lighting system. You will need to choose the one that best suits your needs. If your primary priority is to display plants in your living space, you will want to use a different set-up than if you are establishing a garden room in your basement. To install HID lights in a garden room, you have two basic options. The simplest set-up involves little equipment or time. Simply hang the lamp from an overhead beam or if necessary, construct a simple yet sturdy wooden frame to support the light fixture. Place plants under the light. Remember, HID lights are hot and can easily burn plant tips if they come in contact. Be certain that your plants are *at least* a foot from a 400-watt lamp and 18 to 24 inches from a 1000 watt lamp. If you are using a reflective hood with a diffuser, the lamp can be plased at 18 inches. We recommended that you hang the lamp higher first, then move it down daily. Make sure to check plants daily for signs of heat damage.

We recommend that you purchase a simple pulley kit

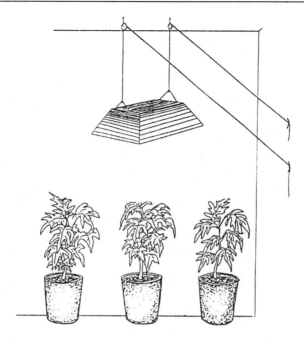

*First hang the light higher above the plants and move it down a few inches a day so plants get used to the light and do not burn. The pulley system makes it very easy to raise and lower the HID.*

or just the components and use the pulley system to hang the lamp(s) over your garden. This method is well worth the time it takes to set up. By hanging your lamps on a pulley system, you can ensure that they are an optimum distance from your garden. Some gardeners simply use hooks in the ceiling and a chain to hang the lamp. To move the lamp up or down, simply hook the chain to a diffrent link. You can also easily move the lamp up out of the way when you want to walk around and enjoy the garden. Some gardeners hang HID lights from the ceiling to light plants on benches and under the benches to light plants on the floor. This allows you to double your garden area.

To hang an HID light, follow the simple instructions listed below. For further detail, read the instructions which accompany your light purchase and call the manufacturer or distributor with any questions.

1.  Hanging HID lamps should be the last step in preparing your garden room.  Remember, most HID bulbs can not be used safely if they have been scratched or cracked.  If you install your lighting system last, you will avoid potentially damaging your system.  Install vents, heating units, moveable walls and any other equipment you need before hanging your HID fixtures.  If you are going to paint your walls with a reflective material, do so before installing your lights.

2.  Choose a location for your lamps where they can hang an absolute minimum of 12 inches (400 watt) and 18 inches (1000 watt) above the tips of the garden.   It is better to hang the lamp at 24 inches (400-watt) and 36 inches (1000-watt) at first and gradually move them downward. The heat generated by the lamp and ballast can potentially damage not only plants, but also your garden room.  Place lamps and ballasts a safe distance from walls or ceilings.  If this is not possible, place a protective, non-flammable material such as metal between the wall and the lamp or ballasts. Ballasts can be cumbersome.  If possible, hang a shelf for your ballast close to the floor in a spot where it will not get wet.  Make sure that electrical cords will not hang close to heat sources.

3.  Mount reflective hood in your chosen location. Use a pulley system described earlier in this section for best results.

4.  Test the outlets in your home to determine approximately how many amps are being drawn from each fuse or breaker switch.  To do this, remove a fuse or turn a breaker off and test each outlet to find out which outlets in the house are off.  All outlets that are off when the

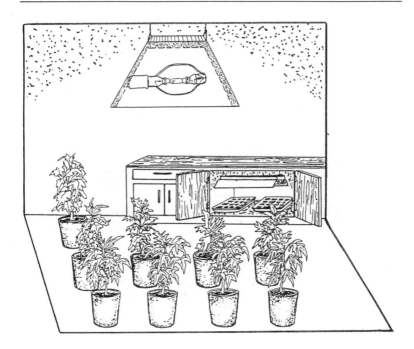

*This gardener is making the most of their space.*

fuse/breaker is off are on the same circuit. Then turn the first fuse or breaker back on and test another circuit. Continue this process until you have determined which outlets go with which circuits. Once you find a circuit that is not used for any other appliances, use this circuit for your lighting system. If you use a 15 or 20 amp circuit, use it for the HID lamp exclusively.

 **Rule of Thumb:** Use only one 1000-watt HID on each 15 or 20 ampere 110-volt circuit. Use only up to two 400 watt HIDs on each 15 or 20 ampere 110-volt circuit.

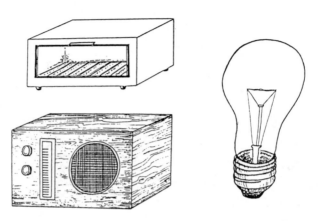

*Add the watts used by a 1400-watt toaster, a 100-watt candescent and a 20 watt radio =   1520 watts/120 = 12.6 amps   This is too many amps to draw on a 15 amp circuit.  You cannot plug your HID into this circuit!*

If you want to use a specific circuit, but it has other appliances on it, plug the appliances into another circuit to make room for the HID light; or find a different circuit for the HID lamp; or install a new circuit.  220-volt circuits make more amps available per circuit.  Do not, replace a 20-amp fuse with a 30-amp fuse.  Always use the proper fuses.  Your wires will overheat, burn and cause a fire.

5.  Once you have selected an appropriate circuit, screw the HID bulb finger-tight into the socket.  Be certain to screw the bulb fully into the socket so that none of the metal base of the bulb shows.  Wipe any smudges off the bulb.

6.  Plug the light plug into the timer, making sure the timer is off.  Plug the timer into a grounded outlet.  Remember, you must use a 3-prong grounded plug.  If you do not have 3-prong outlets in your garden room, buy an

adapter.  Once you set the timer to the desired hours of light per day (photoperiod), you are ready to turn the system on. It will take up to fifteen minutes for your system to reach full brilliance.

NOTE: Check the integrity of all connections period-ically.  Make sure the plug cords fit snugly into outlets.  Poor connections generate excessive heat.  Check the wire con-nections at the ballast.  Check to ensure the bulb is screwed into the socket completely.  Every 3-6 months check the wire connections at the socket.  The heat from the fixture may cause the insulation on the wire to become hard, crack and create a potential short circuit.  For more information, see Appendix C: Troubleshooting the HID

# Chapter Six:
# Electricity and
# Indoor Gardening

## Electricity Basics

Once you have selected a lighting system that best suits your needs, you must know how to install it and how to best maintain it. This chapter provides you with general guidelines to follow when you are installing your HID lighting system. Many successful gardeners use timers, light movers and other electrical equipment to improve their garden output. It is important for gardeners to have a basic understanding of how electricity works. In this chapter you will find explanations of some crucial electrical concepts. Our focus is on how to apply electricity to your lighting and gardening needs. Given our priority of getting the highest return on your growing dollars, we also explore ways in which you can conserve electricity and stretch your electric bill. This chapter does not attempt to cover all the intricacies of electricity. Before you undertake any electrical installation or modification, please consult a reliable source (book or qualified electrician) for further information.

When you are working with electricity, always remember to exercise caution. Working carefully can save you time, money and a potential shock. Always work from the bulb back towards the outlet. Plugging in the cord is the last thing you do. It is a good idea to have ground fault inter-rupter (GFI) outlets that are properly installed. GFI outlets are common in the bathrooms, kitchens and outdoors on new homes. These outlets contain a breaker switch that automatically turns electricity off when it is faulty. The GFI outlet can save you from serious accident if your garden room's electric system becomes unsafe.

 **Rule of Thumb:** Install GFI (ground fault inter-rupter) outlets in your garden room.

WARNING! All artificial light sources use electricity. Water and nutrient solutions are always in close proximity to plants. Water and electricity DO NOT MIX! Do not work on exposed electrical wiring when water is around. Always turn the lighting equipment off and unplug it before mainte-nance. Keep water and nutrient solution well away from all electrical equipment.

Throughout our evaluations of different lighting sys-tems, we have referred to their efficiency in terms of watts. For example, we have compared how many lumens-per-watt each lamp produces. An ampere is one of the measurements that determines a watt. Ohm's power law defines the rela-tionship between volts, amps and resistance. Electric power is usually expressed in watts (watts = volts x amps). An ampere (amp) is a measurement of electrons in motion. Electricity can be measured both by an absolute measure-ment and a measurement of it in motion. A coulomb is an absolute measure of a portion of electricity. When an electri-cal current flows at one coulomb per second, it has one ampere. A volt is a measurement of electrical pressure. You can envision this by comparing volts and amperes to water and a faucet. Volts is like the water pressure, measured in pounds per square inch (PSI) and amperes is the equivalent of water flow in gallons per minute (GPM). Most homes are wired under the pressure of approximately 120 to 220 volts. When you multiply volts by amperes, you get a measurement

of work referred to as a watt.  A watt measures the amount of
electricity flowing in a wire.  1000-watts equals 1 kilowatt.
Understanding watts is important for the hobby gardener
because you do not want to mix watts.  That is to say, you
can not run a 1000-watt lighting system on a 400-watt ballast, or vice versa.  To do so would be an expensive electrical
experiment as you will undoubtedly ruin your lighting system.

 **Rule of Thumb:** Run one 1000-watt lamp per bedroom without an overloading electrical circuits.  For
example, you can run three 1000-watt lamps in a
three bedroom house.

In addition, it is important for gardeners to understand amperes because they measure the amount of electricity traveling through  a given circuit.  When you set up your
lighting system and any other electrical equipment you may
employ in your garden, you do not want to overload a circuit.
In general, use only one 1000-watt HID lamp for each 15 to
20 ampere circuit.  More than that can overload the system
and cause outages; the breaker will trip or the fuse burn out.
A 1000-watt HID lamp uses approximately 9.2 amps of electricity on a regular 120 volt circuit.  Remember, ballasts
draw electricity too.  A 1000-watt halide system actually
draws about 1104 watts including the ballast.  Most homes
have fuse or breaker boxes which will indicate how many
amps of service are available for each fuse or breaker.  Fuses
and breakers can be rated for 15, 20, 25, 30 or 40 amperes.
However, you can not use more than 80 percent of the amps
or you will overload the system.  In general, you can run up
to three 1000-watt lamps without an overload in a 1-3 bedroom house.  Up to five lamps can be operated in a larger
house.  If you need more circuits than are available to you,
contract an electrician.

*Sunglasses will help protect against ultraviolet light.*

Most ultraviolet light is filtered out by the outer envelope of the bulb. However there is some UV light that penetrates through the glass. If you are sensetive to UV light, take precautions when in the garden room. Wear UV-blocking sunglasses and cover skin to protect from UV.

**Safety Notes:** Check the integrety of all connections before turning on the lamp. Make sure that plugs fit snugly into outlets. Also check all connections periodically for heat. If there is excessive heat, there is a poor connection. Also check the wire connections at the balast and check to ensure the bulb is firmly in place. We also reccommend that you check the socket wiring every 3 to 6 months. Sometimes the heat from the fixture will cause the insullation to become hard, crack and create a potential short circuit.

*Water and electricity do not mix!*

1. Operate in a well ventilated area, not in a confined area.
2. Match control gear with correct lamp
3. Do not leave transformer on without lamp operating.
4. Operate ballast box in manufacturer's upright position only.
5. Maximum ambient (room) temperature 35 degrees Celsius.
6. Keep away from moist areas.
7. Turn off switch when replacing lamp.
8. Return to manufacturer for repairs.
9. Operate on safety circuit breakers
10. WARNING: 1,000 to 4,000 volts on lamp lead when starting.
11. DANGER - Leave plug in power point for minimum of one minute after switch off, to allow capacitors to discharge.

**Rule of Thumb:** Operate only one 1000-watt lamp on each 15 to 20 ampere/120 volt circuit.

Be certain to provide a ground for electricity. A ground's function is to connect electricity to the ground or earth for safety reasons. You need a ground in case the electricity travels somewhere it is not supposed to. If the circuit is grounded, the electricity will travel into the earth and be rendered harmless. You can form a ground using a copper wire that runs parallel to the circuit and is attached to a metal ground stake or metal cold water pipe that is buried in the ground. All circuits in your home should be attached to the same ground stake. On most plugs today, you see the ground wire. It is the third wire with the big round prong on a male plug. An HID system must have a ground that runs continuously from the socket through the ballast, the main fuse box and finally to the house ground. The ground wire is usually green or green with a yellow stripe. The other wires are "hot", usually black or brown (the smaller of the two prongs on 120-volt AC plugs) and the other is "common", usually white or blue (the larger of the two prongs of 120-volt AC plugs).

## Energy Conservation

To determine how much a light system will cost to run:, find out how much you pay per kilowatt-hour (KWH) on your electric bill. 1000 watts = 1 KW. a 1000-watt lamp running for one hour = 1 KWH. A 400-watt lamp running for one hour = 0.4 KWH.

For example: if your electricity costs $0.12 per KWH and you are running a 1000-watt lamp 18 hours per day, then:

## Cost of Electricity Chart

| | 12 hour Days | | 18 hour Days | |
|---|---|---|---|---|
| | Day | Month | Day | Month |
| $0.02 . | .24 | 7.20 | .36 | 10.80 |
| $0.03 . | .36 | 10.80 | .54 | 16.20 |
| $0.04 . | .48 | 14.40 | .72 | 21.60 |
| $0.05 | .60 | 18.00 | .90 | 27.00 |
| $0.06 | .72 | 21.60 | 1.08 | 32.40 |
| $0.07 | .84 | 25.20 | 1.26 | 37.80 |
| $0.08 | .96 | 28.80 | 1.44 | 43.20 |
| $0.09 | 1.08 | 32.40 | 1.62 | 48.60 |
| $0.10 | 1.20 | 36.00 | 1.80 | 54.00 |

$0.12 x 18 hours = $2.16 per day
$2.16 x 30 days = $64.80 per month

If electricity costs $0.12 per KWH and you are running a 400-watt lamp 18 hours per day, then:

$0.12 x 0.4 (40% of 1000) = 0.48
  0.48 x 18 hours per day = $0.86 per day
$0.86 x 30 days = $25.80

Understanding electricity can also help you save money. For instance, understanding electrical wire and wiring in general can help you save money. Electrical wire is available in different gauges, (sizes). The smaller the rating, the larger the wire. Most homes are wired with 14-gauge wire. Wire size is important for two reasons: ampacity and voltage (or IR) drop. Ampicity measures the number of amperes a wire is able to carry safely. When electricity flows through wire it creates heat. This heat translates into wasted power. Use the proper thickness of wire (at least 14 gauge) to prevent excess loss of power through heat.

**Rule of Thumb:** Use at least 14 gauge wire on HID lighting systems to maximize lamp efficiency and lower electrical consumption.

If you force too many amps through a wire, it will create heat and a voltage drop. Remember, volts measure electricity under pressure. If you force too small a wire to carry too much electricity, the wire will heat up (perhaps enough to blow a fuse) and the voltage will drop as you move away from the outlet. As electricity travels from the outlet, it generates more heat and has more potential for voltage drops. How does this pertain to your garden room? Voltage drops waste electricity and degrade the efficiency of your lamp. If your lamp is designed to work at 120 volts and it receives only 108 it is receiving only 90 percent of the power it needs to operate efficiently. The light does not, however, emit that same 90 percent. Instead, it produces *only 70 percent* of its intended light. To avoid paying for that wasted electricity, make sure that you use the proper gauge wire. In general, use 14-gauge for all wiring and extension cords up to 60 feet. (However if your power cord is 8 feet or shorter, you can use 16 -gauge wire. For those over 60 feet, use 12-gauge wire. It may be difficult to find these heavier gauge cords, but using 16 or 18 gauge cords will strain the lighting system and reduce it efficiency. Remember, the farther electricity travels, the weaker it becomes and the more heat it produces. To avoid these unnecessary strains on your system, cut your extension cords to the exact length you need.

Understanding ampacity and voltage drops is only one way to conserve energy. Energy and budget-conscious gardeners utilize the heat produced by HIDs during winter months to save on their heating bills. You can also save money on your electricity bill by using power during off-peak hours. Many power companies have to generate a lot of electricity during business hours but are unable to sell such high quantities after hours. Instead of shutting their power plants down and producing less electricity (this would be both impractical and expensive), they offer their power for greatly discounted prices, sometimes as low as one-third the cost of electricity during the day. The more power you use during non-peak hours, the more of a discount you are likely to receive. Utilizing power during off-peak hours is no inconvenience to an indoor gardener. To get the most benefit from artificial lights, many gardeners utilize natural light during the day and begin artificial lighting supplementation at dusk anyway.

## Timers

A timer is an inexpensive investment that will help you to make the most of your HID lights. Plants depend on the same photoperiod each day. To get the best return on your lighting investment, buy a timer to turn your lights on and off at regular intervals. Using a timer ensures that your plants will receive a controlled light period at the same time, for the same duration, each day.

When purchasing a timer for lights, make sure that it is heavy duty, grounded and has the proper amperage and tungsten rating to meet your needs. Some timers have a different amperage rating for the switch; always check for the switch amp rating, it could be lower than that of the timer. For example, Intermatic, makes the HBIIIC, an inexpensive, single light timer with two "on" trippers and two "off" trippers. This timer is adequate for standard HIDs (150 - 1000 watts). If you want a timer capable of controlling more than one HID light system, it must be able to handle more amperage. Dayton is the leading timer manufacturer in the US. This company makes cycle timers that can handle upwards of 40 amperes. You must wire these timers with outlets.

Consult the manufacturer or a qualified electrician to complete wiring for up to four 1000-watt lamps on such a timer.
Other retail companies manufacturer timers that are already
prewired and ready to use for multiple lamp control.

Control only lamps on the lamp timer. Do not add a
pump, heater, fan, etc. to the lamp timer. The other appliances generally have different cycling requirements and the
timer may not handle the extra amperage (load) drawn by
the extra appliances.

Utilizing a timer also allows you to coordinate all of
your garden's equipment. When you bring a garden indoors,
you make a commitment to playing Mother Nature. In so
doing, you are assuming responsibility for the myriad factors
which ensure healthy plant growth— water, light, air circulation, carbon dioxide enrichment, fertilization. Many of
those components can be automated. The better you plan
their coordination, the healthier your garden room will be.
For instance, during hot summer nights when you are using
HID lights, you might also need to provide air circulation
and ventilation to counteract the heat emitted by the lamps.
A timer allows you to maximize the benefit of all of your garden equipment individually and as a coordinated whole.

Note: If you are growing Christmas cactus, chrysan-
tehmums, etc. and want to change a 12 hour photoperiod
from day to night, make sure you run the lamp in a double
dark period (two consecutive 12-hour dark periods). If you
run two 12-hour light periods back to back, flowering will
be delayed.

Always remember to ask how many lights (total
watts) the timer will handle. If you are running more than
2,000 or 3,000 watts, you may want to attach the lamps to a
relay and control the relay with a timer. The advantage of a
relay is it offers a path for more electricity without having to
change the timer.

# Appendix A:
# Light and Radiant Energy

Light is one of many forms of radiant energy. X-rays, radio waves, ultra-violet rays and infrared rays are other examples of radiant energy. Light is the only form of radiant energy that can be detected by the human eye. Humans can not actually see light, but light is the only reason we can see at all. When you look at a plant, you do not see light. However, it is because the plant reflects light that you know it exists.

Light, like all radiant energy, travels through the atmosphere in electromagnetic waves. Picture the ocean with its wave crests and troughs. Electromagnetic waves travel in much the same way, with crests and troughs. Unlike ocean waves which change with seasons, winds and moon cycles, electromagnetic waves travel at a constant speed of 186,000 miles per second in air or in a vacuum. Although all electromagnetic waves travel at the same velocity, they do not all possess an equal amount of energy. Radiant energy is measured in wavelengths, with different wavelengths signifying different amounts of energy. A wavelength is the distance between two adjacent crests or two adjacent troughs. By measuring the wavelengths of radiant energy, scientists have been able to classify and locate the energies in relation to one another on a spectrum.

Light only represents a small portion of the spectrum. In fact, the spectrum is so vast and the wavelengths change so drastically throughout it that scientists employ several different measuring units to classify all the wavelengths. Angstroms, nanometers, millicrons and microns are the units that measure the visible portion of the spectrum. For our purposes, we will use nanometers (nm) which are equivalent to a millionth of a millimeter.

Even within the visible portion of the spectrum, light travels at different wavelengths classified according to color. Light energy ranges from 380 nanometers at the violet end of the visible spectrum to 760 nanometers at the red end. The wavelength of the radiation determines the color of the light. Each color, or wavelength, has a different energy content. This energy is measured in photons. Photons are small packets of energy carried in light's waves. Short wavelengths, such as blue, carry fewer photons, but the energy per photon is much greater than those carried in longer wavelengths such as red. The longer wavelengths have more photons, but each photon has less energy. The wavelength, number of photons and energy per photon determine the amount of radiant energy available for plant use.

To grow well, plants must be supplied with radiant energy that fosters plant food production. Research has shown that plants do not use all the colors of the light spectrum equally or for the same function. For the hobby gardener, understanding how and when a plant responds to a particular color can help you get the most out of your light investment. A plant's radiation source, be it natural or artificial, must provide radiant energy which is useful to the plant. Extra radiation is wasteful. The sun, in fact, is an inefficient source of radiant energy as far as plants are concerned. The sun's radiant energy is made up of a relatively equal distribution of wavelengths. Although the sun's light appears white, it is actually a blend of red, orange, yellow, green, blue and violet. Plants use only a small portion of the sun's energy. Because the sun is free, it can afford to be wasteful. When you pay an electric bill to provide radiant energy to your plants, it is important that you know how to make the most of your lighting dollars.

## Measuring Light

Technically, it is misleading to measure radiant energy for plants in terms of foot-candles, watts-per-square foot or watts-per-square-meter. Horticulturists and lamp manufacturers measure in different units because there is a difference between radiant energy (that's used by plants) and luminous energy (that's visible to humans). Radiant energy, which is energy emitted or received in the form of radiation, is measured in joules or watt-seconds (Ws). One watt is equivalent to one joule per second. Luminous energy refers to the quantity of light radiated or received over a period of time relative to its effect on the human eye. Luminous energy is rated in lumens (lm) or lumen-seconds (lm.s.) Foot-candle measurements are based upon the human eye's sensitivity to light. However, the foot-candle is a useful measurement which can be converted into absolute energy units.

# Appendix B:
# Light Requirements of Plants

## Plant Selection Guide

African violets, begonias and impatiens flower constantly under lights. Begonias of all types, ferns, oxalis, geraniums, annuals, small shrubs and trees such as jasmine, gardenia, crape myrtle, dwarf lantana and dwarf pomegranate, citrus and figs all grow well under HID's.

African Violets, parent plants and cuttings of this short-day plant are given 18 hours of light a day at a level of 2600 lux (260 fc). Flowering is induced with a short 12 to 14-hour photoperiod.

Azalea cuttings propagated under a light level of 2600 lux (260 fc), 18 hours a day grow fast and uniform. Flowers are effectively forced by supplying 3,000 mWms2 for 16 hours a day.

Beans: grow with a light level of 4,000 - 6,000 lux (400-600 fc) for at least 16 hours per day. The more light they get, the stronger and healthier they will grow.

Bedding plants: just about any annual flower that you want to grow will grow super under a HID. Give the small plants a range of 4,000 - 6,000 lux (400-600 fc) for basic growth. Some growers give bedding plants 24 hours of light per day. Once they get a little size, and can take more light, give it to them for super growth.

Begonias: Supplemental lighting promotes cuttings to form on the varieties Rieger, Elatior and Lorraine when natural light is lacking. A light level of 2600 lux (260 fc) is the norm. Use 2600 lux (260 fc) 18 hours a day to nurture young seedlings and to speed flowering. Rooting is stimulated in begonia cuttings by artificial light.

Bromeliads: A light level of 2600 lux (260 fc) 18 hours a day is used to promote stronger growth and the development of seedlings and young plants. On larger bromeliads, supplemental lighting is normally used to help stimulate floral formation. A light level of 2,000 lux (200 fc) for 24 hours a day is used to stimulate flowering. Many times other flower-inducing means are combined with lighting to hasten blooming.

Bulbs can grow with relatively low levels of light, 2,000 - 4,000 lux (200 - 400 fc). There is nothing like bringing bulbs into the house to force. Once the bulb has met its cooling requirement (you can place them in the refrigerator) plant it and place under the HID. You will find the flower on the bulb to be much stronger and last longer.

Cacti and succulents: jade, miniature crassulas, Christmas, Easter and Thanksgiving cactus etc. - are probably the easiest to care for under lights. They require a minimum of care and infrequent watering, but lots of light. In winter when the days are short, cacti greatly benefit from intense supplemental light. A lighting level of 4,000 lux (400 fc) for 18 hours a day will produce phenomenal results in seedlings, cuttings and adult cacti. Some varieties of cactus respond more favorably to 24 hours of light.

Calceolaria: Early flowering is achieved by applying supplemental lighting (1300 lux (130 fc)) for 24 hours a day from bud induction until flowering. Maintain the temperature between 60 and 65 degrees for maximum productivity.

Camelia cuttings and seedlings grow well with 2,000 - 4,000 (200-400 fc) of light. Once the little plants are strong enough to brave the outdoor elements, they can be transplanted.

Carnations, like chrysanthemums, are propagated very successfully by using a parent plant and supplemental light. In fact, side shoots from cut flowers make excellent cuttings. Cuttings are taken and given 16 hours of light (2600 lux (260 fc)). Excessive flowering may occur if more than 16 hours of light per day is permitted. The carnation is a long-day plant, it is possible to light it 24 hours a day to grow more and more profuse flowers. However, after 18 hours of light a day, the extra light produces a minimum of growth.

Chrysanthemums are one of the most responsive flowers to supplemental light in all stages of life. In winter parent plants are given 4,000 lux (400 fc), 20 hours a day. Given lighting during the first month of vegetative growth increases bud count and foliage production. Being a short-day plant, the chrysanthemum requires 20 hours of light a day during the first month of vegetative growth and 12 hours of light (2,000 lux (200 fc) and 12 hours of uninterrupted darkness to flower properly.

Coleus grows well under 2,600 lux (260 fc) of light. To get the super vibrant colors this species is known for, give plants more light. Continue to add light until the colors are at their peak. If too much light is available, colors will fade.

Cucumber seedlings grow exceptionally well under HID lights. Give young seedlings a light level of 4500 mWm2 for the first 10 days of growth for 24 hours a day. After this, shorten the photoperiod to 16 hours per day and increase the light level to 6000 mWm2.

Cyclamen seedlings given supplemental lighting (2600 lux (260 fc)) have more uniform growth and less damping off. The young plants are given 18 hours of light a day.

Endive is easy to propagate when given 2,600 lux. (260 fc) for 16 to 24 hours per day.

Ficus such as the Benjamin fig grow under low light conditions of 2,600 lux (260 fc). Ficus like to receive light 16-18 hours per day for best growth.

Fuchsia will grow under as little as 1,000 lux (100 fc), but will flower more profusely if given more light for at least 16 hours per day.

Geraniums and pelargoniums propagated by seed or

from cuttings greatly benefit from supplemental light. Parent plants are given 18 hours of light at a level of 2600 lux (260 fc) to increase cutting production. The cuttings are given less light but for the same 18 hours a day. Geraniums are a short-day plant and flower with shorter days or colder temperatures. F1 hybrid seed-propagated geraniums can be given 24 hours of light a day at a level of 2600 lux (260 fc) from the beginning of life. These F1 hybrids do not need short days for flower induction.

Gloxinas are given a light level of 6000 mWm2 18 hours a day to enhance growth and development of seedlings and young plants. Give potted gloxinas a light level of 4500 mWm2 to promote large healthy flowers.

Kalanchoe parent plants are given 18 hours of light a day to prevent flowering of this long-day plant. Normally propagated vegetatively, cuttings are given 18 to 24 hours of light at a level of 2600 lux (260 fc). Flowering is induced by giving the plants an equal 12 hours of light and 12 hours of darkness.

Lettuce is lighted at a level of 6000 mWm2 during its entire life. If given a higher level of light, lettuce might bolt.

Lillies can grow with relatively low levels of light, 1,000 - 2,000 lux (100 - 200 fc).  The flower on the bulb to be much stronger and last longer.

Orchids: The blooms and overall growth of many varieties of orchids are greatly enhanced by supplemental lighting during the winter. See: special section below on light requirements of orchids.  Light requirements for orchids fall into three categories.  High: 3000 foot-candles or more, which is equivalent to the amount of light available to plants growing in the middle of a sunny field.  Medium: 1500-3000 foot-candles, which is similar to the amount of light received by lightly shaded plants.  Low: under 1500 foot-candles, for plants that grow deep beneath the canopy of the forest. Orchids can be referred to as being high light, cool-air plants. The Cymbidium is a good example of this type of orchid. The Phalaenopsis genus is a low-light, warm-air orchid.

Peppers grow very well under HID light. They will grow in as little as 4,000 lux (400fc), but grow much better when given more light. Peppers respond best when given 24 hours of HID light.

Roses love light. Miniature roses grow incredibly well under HID light. Levels of 2600 lux (260 fc), 24 hours per day will greatly increase flower yield, size and quality. Supplemental carbon dioxide really boost growth of these super-productive roses.

Snapdragons are a favorite fall and early spring flower. There are two genetically different types of snapdragons short-day, referred to as Group I or II or "winter flowering," and long-day, referred to as Group III or IV or "summer flowering." When setting this plant out for early spring blooms, give seedlings supplementary lighting at a level of 4,000 lux (400 fc) so that a day length of 16 hours is reached. This will speed flowering by about four weeks. In fact, even better results can be achieved by giving long-day plants 24 hours of light (2,000 lux (200 fc)) throughout their life. Short day snapdragons should receive short 12 hour days after they are about two months old for maximum blooming potential.

Strawberries are a fun crop to grow under HIDs. They produce very well and can grow with a minimum of light, about 2,000 lux (200 fc). The more light they are given, the better they set fruit.

Tomatoes, peppers and eggplants flourish under HID light. The more light these plants are given the bigger they grow and the more fruit they produce. Give these plants 4,000 lux (400 fc) as soon the first true leaves appear and maintain the light level at a minimum throughout their entire life. Give tomatoes 18 hours of light per day.

# Appendix C: Troubleshooting the HID

**Always disconnect power from the ballast before troubleshooting HID system.**

1. If you run into trouble with an HID system always talk to the distributor you bought it from first.
2. If your system is covered under waranty, call the distributor before attempting any repairs yourself.. You may void your waranty.
3. Always unplug your system before inspecting.
4. Allow the bulb to fully cool before touching.

## Common Ballast Problems
1. If the ballast is too noisy, it may be due to an old transformer, or loose internal components. You can also dampen noise by isolating the ballast. Replace transformers every 5 - 7 years.
2. If the ballast is smelly, transformer resins may be burning off. If smell persists, unplug ballast and contact your distributor.
3. If the ballast is smoky, unplug ballast and contact your distributo;r there may have been a fire in the ballast or melting components.

## Bulbs
1. Some flickering is normal in lamps. Allow time for them to stabilize. Have older flickering lamps inspected by the supplier.
Dim lamps are most often the result of old bulbs or faulty capacitors.
3. If your bulb starts, then fails repeatedly, its life is over.

Time to replace lamp.

## Capacitors

1. If the capacitor appears to be leaking or is swolen, replace it. Unplug the ballast immediately.
2. Always discharge metal "oil-filled" capacitors with a ruffer handled tool before touching. Capacitors can hold an electrical charge for a long time. They are dangerous when charged. We reccommend that you take the entire ballast into the supplier for servicing.

## Ignitors

1. Igniters are only found in HP sodium systems.
2. If it appears burned or mishapen, replace it.

## Sockets

If the ceramic portion of the socket is cracked or broken, it should be replaced. Allow bulb to fully cool before removing it from the xocket.

## Electrical Cords

1. Replace cords if there any signs of heat damage. Unplug the ballast immediately. Exercise caution.
NOTE: Failure of any component in a HID system can result in lamp failure. Contact your HID distributor if any problems arise.

## Power Supply

1 Check all connections to ensure they are secure.
2. Look for signs of heat (burned wires, melted wire, etc.)
3. Check fuses and breaker switches
4. Replace or repair inadequate connections.
5. Take system to retailer if burning of fixtures occurs.

# Appendix D:
# Other Bulbs

## Incandescent Lamps

Common for household lighting, incandescents are popular because their initial cost is low, but they are inefficient. Before the invention of plant growth lamps, incandescents were popularly used in combination with cool white fluorescents. Today, however, with the array of lighting options available to gardeners, incandescents are rarely used.

"Wonderlite" is the only incandescent we recommend for horticultural use. Incandescent bulbs convert only 6 to 9 percent of electric energy into visible light and release the rest as heat. The expected life of common incandescent bulbs is very short, except for the "Wonderlite". In addition, although incandescent bulbs provide sufficient red light for plant growth, they are not a good source of blue light. Therefore, they do not efficiently stimulate photosynthesis. In fact, they produce leggy, elongated plants. See *The New Revised Gardening Indoors* by George F. Van Patten for a complete discussion on incandescent bulbs.

## Tungsten Halogens

Halogen bulbs were invented in 1958 for use as landing lights on jet airplanes. They are used today as car headlights and similar applications. Tungsten halogens, like incandescents, are not a cost-effective choice for indoor gardening needs. Initial investment is less with a tungsten halogen but operating costs quickly eat up any initial savings. Their lumen-per-watt output is very low with only 10-15 percent of the energy they produce falling in the visible light range. Tungsten halogen light output is concentrated in the far red range of the spectrum, making the light inefficient for photosynthesis and plant growth. They also have a relatively short life. See *The New Revised Gardening Indoors* by George F. Van Patten for a complete discussion on tungsten halogens.

## Fluorescent Lamps

Gardeners are divided on their opinions about fluorescent lighting. Some gardeners feel that their disadvantages outweigh their benefits, while others employ fluorescents with excellent results. One thing is certain. Fluorescents are more efficient, last longer and are cooler than their incandescent counterparts. Standard fluorescents have a fair lumen-per-watt conversion and are about three times more efficient in converting electrical energy to light than incandescents. Fluorescents have an energy conversion efficiency of 80-85 lumens per watt. For the first 100 hours of use, many fluorescents will produce about ten percent more light then their rated value indicates. After approximately 100 hours, the bulb should stabilize and produce at its rated value. In addition, fluorescent bulbs last up to 10-15 times longer than incandescents.

Until the development of HIDs, fluorescents were popularly used by indoor gardeners. Although fluorescents produce light in both the blue and red spectrums, they do not reach high enough irradiance levels to be useful for photosynthesis. Because HID bulbs are more efficient for general garden purposes, fluorescents today are used mostly for photoperiodic lighting and for seedlings and cuttings.

See *Gardening Indoors with Fluorescent Lights* by George F. Van Patten and Alyssa F. Bust for complete discussion of the lamps.

# Appendix E:
# Conversions to Metric

**Metric Conversion Chart - Approximations**

| When You Know | Multiply by | To Find |
|---|---|---|
| **Length** | | |
| millimeters | 0.04 | inches |
| centimeters | 0.39 | inches |
| meters | 3.28 | feet |
| kilometers | 0.62 | miles |
| inches | 25.40 | millimeters |
| inches | 2.54 | centimeters |
| feet | 30.48 | centimeters |
| yards | 0.91 | meters |
| miles | 1.16 | kilometers |
| **Area** | | |
| square centimeters | 0.16 | square inches |
| square meters | 1.20 | square yards |
| square kilometers | 0.39 | square miles |
| hectares | 2.47 | acres |
| square inches | 6.45 | square centimeters |
| square feet | 0.09 | square meters |
| square yards | 0.84 | square meters |
| square miles | 2.60 | square kilometers |
| acres | 0.40 | hectares |
| **Volume** | | |
| milliliters | 0.20 | teaspoons |
| milliliters | 0.60 | tablespoons |

| milliliters | 0.03 | fluid ounces |
|---|---|---|
| liters | 4.23 | cups |
| liters | 2.12 | pints |
| liters | 1.06 | quarts |
| liters | 0.26 | gallons |
| cubic meters | 35.32 | cubic feet |
| cubic meters | 1.35 | cubic yards |
| teaspoons | 4.93 | milliliters |
| tablespoons | 14.78 | milliliters |
| fluid ounces | 29.57 | milliliters |
| cups | 0.24 | liters |
| pints | 0.47 | liters |
| quarts | 0.95 | liters |
| gallons | 3.790 | liters |

**Mass and Weight**

| grams | 0.035 | ounce |
|---|---|---|
| kilograms | 2.21 | pounds |
| ounces | 28.35 | grams |
| pounds | 0.45 | kilograms |

1 inch (in.) = 25.4 millimeters (mm)
1 foot (12 in.) = 0.3048 meters (m)
1 yard (3 ft) = 0.9144 meters
1 mile = 1.60937 kilometers
1 square inch = 645 square millimeters
1 square foot = 0.0929 square meters
1 square yard = 0.8361 square meters
1 square mile = 2.59 square kilometers

**Liquid Measure Conversion**
1 pint (UK) = 0.56824 liters
1 pint dry (US) = 0.55059 liters
1 pint liquid (US) = 0.47316 liters
1 gallon (UK) (8 pints) = 4.5459 liters

1 gallon dry (US) = 4.4047 liters
1 pint liquid (US) = 3.7853 liters

1 ounce = 28.3495 grams
1 pound (16 ounces) = 0.453592 kilograms

1 gram = 15.4325 grains
1 kilogram = 2.2046223 pounds

1 millimeter = 0.03937014 inches (UK)
1 millimeter = 0.03937 invhrd (US)
1 centimeter = 0.3937014 inches (UK)
1 centimeter = 0.3937 inches (US)
1 meter = 3.280845 feet (UK)
1 meter = 3.280833 feet (US)
1 kilometer = 0.6213722 miles

**Celsius to Fahrenheit**
Celsius temp. x (9/5 = 32) = Fahrenheit
Fahrenheit temp. -32, 5/9 x remainder = Celsius

**Light Conversion**
1 footcandle = 10.76 = lux
1 lux = 0.09293
Lux = 1 lumen/square meters

# Glossary

This Glossary contains many very simple and some not so simple words in the context of their usage in this book. Many examples are given to promote good indoor horticultural practices.

Alternating Current (AC) - an electric current that reverses its direction at regularly occurring intervals. Homes have AC.

Ampere (amp) - the unit used to measure the strength of an electric current: A 20-amp circuit is overloaded when drawing more than 17 amps.

Arc - luminous discharge of electricity (light) between two electrodes.

Arc tube- container for luminous gases also houses the arc.

Average Life - is the point at which 50 percent of the bulbs in a test fail to ignite.

BT - Blown Tubular, or the shape reference of HID bulbs. A BT-37 has a smaller bulb than a BT-56.

BU - bulb is to be operated in a base up position.

BD - bulb is to be operated in the base down position.

Ballast - the sum of the transformer, capacitor and connecting wiring in metal halide systems. HP sodium systems require a transformer, capacitor and an ignitor. Iwasaki Ignitron bulbs have their own built-in starter.

Breaker box - electrical circuit box having on/off switches rather than fuses.

Bulb - 1. the outer glass envelope or jacket that protects the arc tube of an HID lamp 2. clove or bulb of garlic.

Burning Position

Carbohydrate - neutral compound of carbon, hydrogen and oxygen. Sugar, starch and cellulose are carbohydrates.

Chlorophyll- the green photosynthetic matter of plants: Chlorophyll is found in the chloroplasts of a cell.

Circuit - a circular route traveled by electricity.

Color spectrum - the band of colors (measured in nm) emitted by a light source.

Color Temperature - is expressed in degrees Kelvin. It is a unit of measurement to show the color (spectrum) of light emitted by a lamp. The back of this book has a chart that shows the color of light at different degrees Kelvin.

Common - the common wire is normally white in a 110 volt system.

Core - the transformer in the ballast is referred to as a core.

Direct Current (DC) - an electric current that flows in only one direction

Dome - the part of the HID outer bulb opposite the neck and threads.

Dome support - the spring-like brackets that mount the arc tube within the outer envelope.

Electrode - a conductor used to establish electrical arc or contact with non-metallic part of circuit.

Envelope - outer protective bulb or jacket of a lamp.

Equinox - the point at which the sun crosses the equator and day and night are each 12 hours long: The equinox occurs twice a year.

Extension cord - extra electrical cord that must be 14-gauge or larger (i.e. 12- or 10-gauge).

Fixture - electrical fitting used to hold electric components.

Flat white - very reflective, whitest white paint available.

Fluorescent lamp - electric lamp using a tube coated with fluorescent material, which has low lumen and heat output: A fluorescent lamp is excellent for rooting cuttings.

Flux - is the unit that measures the rate of flow when light energy moves across a predetermined area.

Footcandle is a unit of illumination equal to the intensity of one candle at a distance of one foot. One f.c. is equal to 10.76 LUX.

Frequency

Fuse - electrical safety device consisting of a metal that MELTS and interrupts the circuit when circuit is overloaded.

Fuse box- box containing fuses that control electric circuits.

Halide - binary compound of a (halogens) with an electropositive element(s).

Halogen - any of the elements fluorine, chlorine, bromine, iodine and astatine existing in a free state: Halogens are in the arc tube of a halide lamp.

Hertz (Hz) - a unit of a frequency that cycles one time each second: A home with a 60 hertz AC current cycles 60 times per second.

HID - High Intensity Discharge.

Hood - reflective cover of a HID lamp: A large, white HOOD is very reflective.

HOR - The abbreviation stamped on some HID bulbs meaning they may be burned in a horizontal position.

Horizontal - parallel to the horizon, ground or floor.

Hot spot - a very bright small area under reflective hoods. A hot spot causes uneven growth.

Ignitor - is used to start HP sodium bulbs.

Illuminance - is the luminous flux density meassured as it falls on a given surface. It is expressed as lumen-per-square-meter (lm/m2).

Inert - chemically non-reactive: Inert growing mediums make it easy to control the chemistry of the nutrient solution.

Initial lumens - is the amount of light measured when the HID lamp has been burning for 100 hours.

Intensity - the magnitude of light energy per unit: Intensity diminishes the farther away from the source.

Irradiance - is the radiant flux density mesaured as it falls on a given surface. Irradiance is expressed in mili-watts-per square-meter (mW/m2) or watts-per-square-meter (W/m2)

Jacket - protective outer bulb or envelope of lamp.

Kilowatt-hour - measure of electricity used per hour: A 1000-watt HID uses one kilowatt per hour.

KV - Kilovolt

Lead = Hot wire

Light mover - a device that moves a lamp back and forth across the ceiling of a garden room to provide more even distribution of light.

Lumen - measurement of light output: One lumen is equal to the amount of light emitted by one candle that falls on one square foot of surface located one foot away from one candle.

Luminous Flux - is measured by lumens (lm). It is the rate of light emission. It is derived by weighing the radiation and mesuring it in relation to the human eye.

Lux - (lx) is the international unit of illumination that describes the quantity of light that falls on one meter from a single point source. One fc = 10.75 lx

Mean - average throughout life: HID's are rated in mean lumens.

Millimeter - thousandth of a meter approximately 04. inch.

Mili-watts-per-meter-squared - is the total amount of light that falls on the area measured.

Monochromatic - producing only one color: LP sodium lamps are monochromatic.

Nanometer - 000001. meter, nm is used as a scale to measure electromagnetic wave lengths of light: Color and light spectrums are expressed in nanometers (nm).

Neck - tubular glass end of the HID bulb, attached to the threads.

Ohm's Power Law - a law that expresses the strength of an electric current: Volts times Amperes equals watts.

Overload - load to excess: A 20-amp circuit drawing 17 amps is overloaded.

POM - mogul socket abreviation used for HOR bulbs - Position Oriented Mogul

POMB - Position Oriented Mogul base - see POM.

Phosphor coating - internal bulb coating that diffuses light and is responsible for various color outputs.

Photoperiod - the relationship between the length of light and dark in a 24-hour period.

Photosynthesis - the building of chemical compounds (carbohydrates) from light energy, water and carbon dioxide.

Phototropism - the specific movement of a plant part toward a light source.

Pigment - The substance in paint or anything that absorbs light, producing (reflecting) the same color as the pigment.

Power surge - interruption or change in flow of electricity.

Radient Energy - is energy emitted, transferred or received in the form of radiation. Joules (J) and watt-seconds (Ws) are the units of measurement that measure radiant energy.

Radiant Flux - is the rate of flow of all energy from any source of radiation. Joules per second (J/x,watt(W) is the unit of measurement that describes radiant flux.

Rejuvenate - Restore youth: A mature plant, having completed its life cycle (flowering), may be stimulated by a new 18 hour photoperiod, to rejuvenate or produce new vegetative growth.

Short circuit - condition that results when wires cross and for m. a circuit. A short circuit will blow fuses.

Socket - threaded, wired holder for a bulb.

Square feet (sq. ft.) - length (in feet) times width equals square feet.

Stroboscopic effect - a quick pulsating or flashing of a lamp.

Synthesis - production of a substance, such as chlorophyll, by uniting light energy and elements or chemical compounds.

Transformer - a devise in the ballast that transforms electric current from one voltage to another.

Tungsten - a heavy, hard metal with a high melting point which conducts electricity well: Tungsten is used for a filament in tungsten halogen lamps.

Ultraviolet - light with very short wave lengths, out of the visible spectrum.

Vertical - up and down perpendicular to the horizontal.

U - Universal burning position of a bulb 360 degrees.

Warm up Time

Watts-per-square-meter (m2)

# Index

## Gardening Indoors with $CO_2$

96 pages - illustrated - 5 1/2" x 8 1/2" - **$12.95**
Packed with the latest information about carbon dioxide enrichment - how to get the most out of $CO_2$ generators and emitters available today. Easy step-by-step instructions on setting up $CO_2$ in your garden room. Double your harvest with $CO_2$ .

## Gardening Indoors with Cuttings

96 pages - illustrated - 5 1/2" x 8 1/2" - **$12.95**
Growing cuttings is fun and easy. This book is loaded with the most productive methods and information. Take cuttings to control plant growth and achieve super yields. Easy step-by-step instructions teach beginners and experts alike how-to take perfect cuttings.

## Gardening Indoors with HID Lights

168 pages - illustrated - 5 1/2" x 8 1/2" - **$14.95**
This book is the definitive book on high intensity discharge (HID) lighting and plant growth. This book overflows with the latest information on high-tech lights. If you use HIDs, you must have this book.

## Gardening Indoors with Rockwool

128 pages - illustrated - 5 1/2" x 8 1/2" - **$14.95**
New and updated volume of *Gardening: The Rockwool Book*. It is reformatted and packed with the latest information on rockwool.

---

| | | |
|---|---|---|
| New Revised Gardening Indoors | **$19.95** | *Shipping, handling & insurance $3 per book* |
| Gardening Indoors With Rockwool | **$14.95** | |
| Gardening Indoors With Cuttings | **$12.95** | |
| Gardening Indoors With HID Lights | **$14.95** | *Call for shipping costs for more than 2 books.* |
| Gardening Indoors With $CO_2$ | **$12.95** | |
| Shipping, handling & insurance (per book) | **$3.00** | |

Ship to: _____

Address _____

City _____ State _____ Zip _____

Telephone _____

Checks & Money Orders only

***Wholesale Clients Wanted***

# Orders (510) 236-3360

## Van Patten Publishing

38912 NE Borin Road, Washougal, WA 98671-9527

## Gardening Indoors with $CO_2$

96 pages - illustrated - 5 1/2" x 8 1/2" - **$12.95**

Packed with the latest information about carbon dioxide enrichment - how to get the most out of $CO_2$ generators and emitters available today. Easy step-by-step instructions on setting up $CO_2$ in your garden room. Double your harvest with $CO_2$.

## Gardening Indoors with Cuttings

96 pages - illustrated - 5 1/2" x 8 1/2" - **$12.95**

Growing cuttings is fun and easy. This book is loaded with the most productive methods and information. Take cuttings to control plant growth and achieve super yields. Easy step-by-step instructions teach beginners and experts alike how-to take perfect cuttings.

## Gardening Indoors with HID Lights

168 pages - illustrated - 5 1/2" x 8 1/2" - **$14.95**

This book is the definitive book on high intensity discharge (HID) lighting and plant growth. This book overflows with the latest information on high-tech lights. If you use HIDs, you must have this book.

## Gardening Indoors with Rockwool

128 pages - illustrated - 5 1/2" x 8 1/2" - **$14.95**

New and updated volume of *Gardening: The Rockwool Book*. It is reformatted and packed with the latest information on rockwool.